-4-

112+
130+
131+
188
335

#407
C133
C189
C229
C306

Jeweled Garden

Jeweled Garden

A COLORFUL HISTORY OF GEMS, JEWELS, AND NATURE

Suzanne Tennenbaum
and Janet Zapata

The Vendome Press

New York

Dedicated to those who contribute to the artistry and preservation of fine jewelry.

First published in the United States of America in 2006 by
The Vendome Press
1334 York Avenue
New York, NY 10021

The publisher wishes to thank Suzanne Tennenbaum for her generous contribution to the publication of this book.

ISBN-10: 0-86565-172-8
ISBN-13: 978-0-86565-172-2

Library of Congress Cataloging-in-Publication Data
   Tennenbaum, Suzanne.
   Jeweled garden : a colorful history of gems, jewelry,
   and nature / Suzanne Tennenbaum and Janet Zapata.
          p.   cm.
   Includes bibliographical references.
   Summary: "Explores the evolution of garden-inspired
   jewelry with 375 full-color photographs from the
   nineteenth century to present day, displaying important
   pieces from world-famous jewelers, including Cartier,
   Tiffany, Mauboussin, Bulgari, Van Cleef & Arpels, and
   Verdura"—Provided by publisher.
   ISBN-13: 978-0-86565-172-2 (hardcover : alk. paper)
   ISBN-10: 0-86565-172-8 (hardcover : alk. paper)
   1. Jewelry—History—20th century—Themes, motives.
   2. Jewelry—History—19th century—Themes, motives.
   3. Decoration and ornament—Plant forms. I. Zapata,
   Janet. II. Title.
   NK7310.T36 2006
   391.709—dc22
                            2006009804

Designer: Judy Hudson
Editor: Sarah Davis

Printed in China

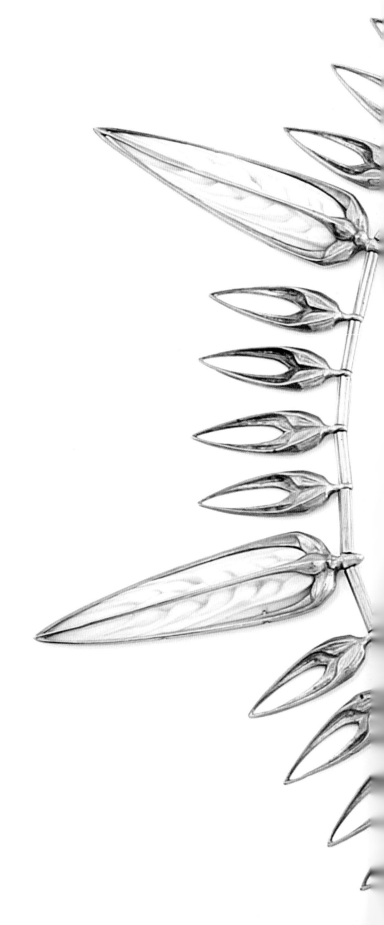

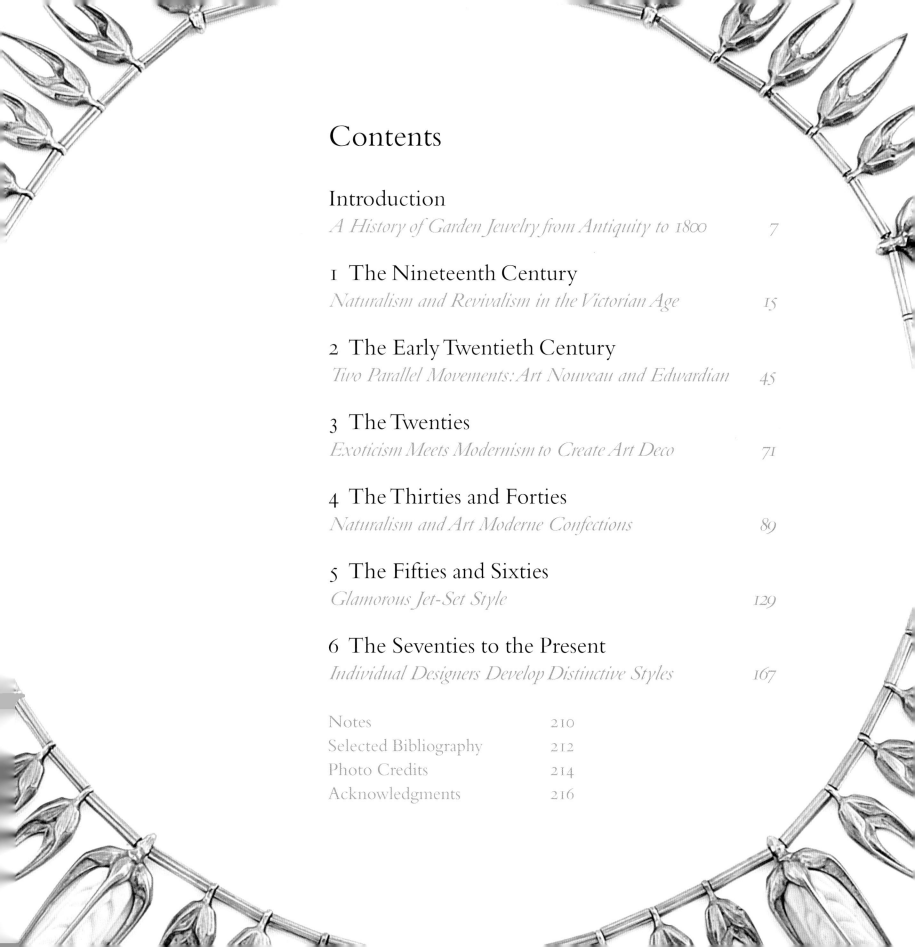

Contents

This chaplet of gold beech leaves with lapis and carnelian beads was found in the cemetery at Ur. It dates between 2600 to 2500 BC. The Metropolitan Museum of Art, New York.

Introduction

A History of Garden Jewelry from Antiquity to 1800

Although no one can say how prehistoric man adorned himself, it seems reasonable to assume that he turned to his immediate environment to fashion items such as simple necklaces or head ornaments woven out of leaves and vines. We do know that, when man began to live in organized communities, he created precious-metal jewelry in plant forms that were worn for their magical significance, symbolic meanings, or apotropaic qualities. Examination of extant pieces shows that great care was taken in the execution of these highly regarded objects. Although silver, lapis lazuli, and carnelian were used in jewelry construction, it was gold, a metal that may have come from the highlands of Turkey and Iran,[1] that was held in the highest esteem. For the most part, until the Hellenistic period, jewelry was made entirely out of gold. Because of its malleability, it could be fashioned into naturalistic plant forms with thin sheets shaped into delicate flower petals and leaves and thin wires replicating the curves of stems.

Some of the earliest known examples of jewelry with botanical motifs date to the third millennium B.C. when the Sumerians occupied Ur, the most powerful city-state in Mesopotamia. Since this advanced society produced the first writing, it is understandable why their jewelry exhibits a highly refined and realistic reproduction of natural forms. The unearthing of the royal tombs yielded headdresses that were made with gold willow and beech leaves with clearly demarcated veins (opposite). At a later date, a stylized flower motif with up to thirteen petals became the distinctive motif of this culture.

But it was the ancient Egyptians who attached great symbolic meanings to most things in their environment, especially plant life. Since their land was so arid, the green of fresh vegetation represented new life

Below top: A pair of Roman gold grape bunch earrings, dating from the 2nd or 3rd century AD, are set with garnets. The Walters Art Museum, Baltimore. Below bottom: Two Egyptian gold rings with lotus motifs include (top) one dating from the Middle Kingdom, 20th to 18th century BC, with lapis and carnelian and (bottom) the other, from the New Kingdom, 16th to the 11th century BC, with blue and white glass. The Walters Art Museum, Baltimore.

Opposite: This Greek gold oak leaf wreath dates to about 350–325 BC. Toledo Museum of Art.

and, by extension, resurrection, exemplified by the papyrus plant. The lotus, the most ubiquitous image in Egypt, was revered because its emergence from the water at sunrise and closing at sunset linked it to the sun. The representation of this plant in jewelry was often set with colored gemstones including feldspar, lapis, and carnelian or colored glass which, when set into gold, resembled enameling (bottom left).

In ancient Greece, botanical imagery played a dominant role in jewelry design from the Classical through Hellenistic periods. Floral and leafy scrolls, palmettes and stylized rosettes were worn in combination with filigree decoration. Elaborate necklaces were strung with seed-like appendages that were often interspersed with female heads. Perhaps the most spectacular Grecian naturalistic jewels were the golden wreaths incorporating countless flowers and leaves. Made up of stems in the form of tapering tubes with acanthus leaves, olive leaves, laurel leaves, or oak leaves joined to it, these representations symbolized heaven, peace, victory, and strength (opposite). They were given as prizes for champions or as offerings to the gods and were also used as funerary jewelry.

Fillets, worn from early Greek to late Roman times, were simpler versions of wreaths made of thin gold, cut to resemble leaves with wires for stems. They were given by the state as a mark of honor or worn in religious processions. Also popular in ancient Rome were necklaces of multiple gold leaf ornaments linked together, and earrings with rosettes from which grape clusters hung (top left). Since agricultural images represented prosperity, cornucopia, corn-measures, and fruits of the harvest such as corn were engraved into gems on seals, an object used to impress the owner's mark.

For the most part, jewelry with botanical representations took a hiatus until the Gothic period in the twelfth century when cloak clasps, belts, and girdles were decorated with acanthus leaf or rosette motifs and crowns were highlighted with fleur-de-lis, a heraldic device based on the floral segments of an iris, tied by an encircling band.

By the second half of the sixteenth century, botanical treatises expounded the virtues of plants in the decorative arts such as those by Bernard Palissy, a ceramicist working for Catherine de Médicis, whose ideas were translated into jewelry design.[2] This fascination with the natural world coincided with an interest in embellishing jewelry not only with colored gemstones but also with enameling. Color became paramount, especially in important commissions such as the Hohenlohe collar fashioned out of enameled twigs from which was suspended a pendant of a white double rose with green enameled branches, a favorite motif of the period.[3] Watch cases, perhaps the most decorative jeweled form of the period, were enameled with flowers[4] or fashioned into flower shapes such as tulips that were decorated with champlevé enamel.[5] The shapes of many pomanders, small cases that held aromatic scents, took the form of fruit such as pears, apples, or melons and were often enameled with floral scenes.[6] Magnificent gemstones were cut into special shapes such as a tourmaline-rubellite sculpted into the guise of a raspberry whose

Right: This bouquet of flowers in white and colored diamonds and emeralds mounted in gold and silver is set *en tremblant* in which the flowers move when worn. It was part of the Russian crown jewels in the latter half of the eighteenth century. Diamond Fund, Moscow, Kremlin.

Below: A 226-carat tourmaline-rubellite in the form of a raspberry with leaves and stem of guilloché with transparent green enamel was created in Europe and given to Catherine the Great by Gustav III of Sweden in 1777. Diamond Fund, Moscow, Kremlin.

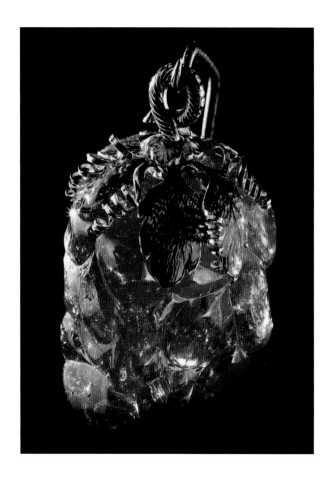

leaves were executed in guilloché with transparent green enamel, a technique of cutting abstract patterns into the surface which is then enameled (opposite, left).[7]

Until the seventeenth century, jewelry had been worn mostly by men as a sign of dignity, but the emphasis now shifted to the adornment of women. It was the beginning of the modern age with fashion dictating the design of jewelry. In place of confining, stiff dresses, a looser cut was adopted using softer fabrics in light colors; concurrently, the décolletage was introduced to show off the feminine figure. Hair was worn open, providing room for sprays or aigrettes of jeweled flowers. During the Baroque period, botanical imagery dominated, as epitomized by the breast ornament which was based on leaf assemblies made up of vine work with a grouping of stones reminiscent of a flower at the center. This style, called *cosse-de-pois* or pea pod, is seen in the engraved designs of Balthasar Lemercier and Jacques Caillart of Paris and Peter Symony of Strasbourg.[8]

By the eighteenth century, the breast ornament had evolved into the stomacher, a triangular jewel that hung from the décolletage to the waistline and was designed with a rosette-like center with a cluster setting and leafy scrolls. The rococo era also witnessed the introduction of the watch with a chatelaine hanging from the waist band, which became the most important daytime jewelry during this period. It could be repoussé chased with figures and leafy scrolls or gem-set with flowers (page 12).

Left: This basket-of-flowers brooch, set with rose diamonds and mounted into silver, was made in France, c. 1770.

Below: This pair of Russian earrings in the form of cherries with Brazilian diamonds was commissioned by Catherine the Great. All the tzarinas and grand duchesses wore these earrings on their wedding day. Diamond Fund, Moscow, Kremlin.

By the second half of the eighteenth century, flowers were everywhere, as seen in the bouquet bodice ornaments that could be eight inches in length. They were composed of an assortment of flowers, held together by a bow, and were often enameled or set with colored gemstones or diamonds. The larger flower heads were set on springs, a style known as *en tremblant*, so that they "trembled" when the wearer moved. Necklaces of garlands of flowers were also popular, as were aigrettes of sprigs arranged in the hair.

But perhaps the one form that is most strongly associated with this period is the *giardinetti* or "little garden" rings whose colored gemstone flowers motifs were arranged in baskets, vases, and pots.[9] A variation on this theme is a brooch with rose-cut diamond flowers arranged asymmetrically in a basket; the diamonds set into collet settings, circular bands of metal that enclosed the stone (p. 11). By the end of the century, the "marquise" style, the shape derived from the laurel leaf of classical jewelry, was faced with an enameled plate, surrounded by a border of diamonds and set with a diamond sprig of flowers (below).

By the end of the eighteenth century, as the neo-classical style replaced the rococo, flowers, once again, took on symbolic meanings, such as the rose that denoted love, but also with the caveat of heartbreak as seen on a pendant with the inscription, *Jamais la rose, sans l'epine* (Never the rose without the thorn) (right). It is fitting that a rose motif ends the eighteenth century since it is the one flower that will dominate botanical jewelry design over the next two centuries.

Finely carved coral berries spring from a band of three-color gold on this English tiara, c. 1845. The gold is worked with a fine tool to resemble leaves. Toledo Museum of Art.

CHAPTER ONE

The Nineteenth Century

Naturalism and Revivalism in the Victorian Age

In the nineteenth century an explosion in design and technology eclipsed any previous period in jewelry history. This was especially evident in the most pervasive, as well as popular, guiding theme of jewelry: flowers, fruits, vegetables, and trees. Although botanical imagery was not a new inspirational source—it had been part of jewelry repertoire since ancient times—the variety of motifs and designs was so prolific that these images became emblematic of the century, bringing a breath of fresh air in contrast to the historic styles.

It was indeed a time of excitement in jewelry design, spurred on by a new middle class that wanted to emulate the aristocracy by wearing the trappings associated with social rank and affluence. This new class was eager to own and, more important, to wear the latest styles, encouraging jewelers to compete with new ideas and designs to fill the need. This century marked the beginning of the modern age in jewelry design, when jewelry became more than just a mark of status: the design of a jewel for its own sake became paramount. Nowhere was this more evident than in jewelry fashioned in the guise of flowers and other delights of the garden.

By the beginning of the nineteenth century, two-dimensional representations, almost abstract in conception, of the eighteenth century evolved into three-dimensional designs conceived in a realistic manner. The restoration of the Bourbon monarchy in France in 1814 ushered in a renewed interest in floral jewelry that lasted throughout the century, gradually evolving from diamond-set sprays to full-color enamel and colored gemstone-set flowers conceived as if freshly cut from the garden.

Many factors contributed to the rise of floral and vegetal jewelry in the nineteenth century. Chief among them was a strong interest in botany and horticulture in the early part of the century. As Charlotte Gere explains in *Victorian Jewelry Design*, "The idea of the flower garden as a place where plants might be cultivated purely for their decorative qualities as distinct from their medicinal or nutritive value was a comparatively recent one, and its wide adoption during the eighteenth century stimulated public interest in flowering garden plants."[1] This spurred many well-to-do gardeners to collect new species of flowers, even traveling to foreign lands in search of new varieties.

The development of the hothouse in an indirect way also contributed to a surge in botanically inspired jewelry. Flowers could be grown in all seasons, no matter how unfavorable the outside weather. This encouraged the importation of new species into Europe and England from such far-away lands as Turkey, India, China, Japan, and North and South America. These flowers that, today, are commonplace garden plants, included the azalea, bleeding heart, chrysanthemum, dahlia, gardenia, hydrangea, magnolia, petunia, rhododendron, tiger lily, wisteria, and new types of roses from China. There was also experimentation in creating new, hardier species of plants such as the pansy and iris whose modern varieties were developed around 1840. The mania for floral jewelry also extended to common flowers and plants native to the West, such as the geranium, fuchsia, sweet pea, and holly.[2]

The nineteenth century also saw the rise of books, encyclopedias, and guides to decorative design, which touted the use of plant design in the decorative arts. Owen Jones's *The Grammar of Ornament*, published in 1856, and Christopher Dresser's *Art of Decorative Design*, published in 1862, both discuss how plants and flowers could be used as the basis for design. But the books that were the most influential on floral jewelry were those focusing on what was known during the Victorian era as "the language of flowers," in which flowers and plants connoted specific meanings. Perhaps the best known of these was *The Language of Flowers*, written by the children's book illustrator Kate Greenaway, published in 1884, which lists flowers and plants and their human-like attributes. This book became very popular both in England and the United States.

The language of flowers, sometimes called *floriography*, was a means of communication in which various flowers and floral arrangements were used to send coded messages, allowing individuals to express feelings they might not be comfortable verbalizing explicitly. Roses were assigned several such sentiments: Red roses conveyed love and beauty; white roses meant "I am worthy of you"; yellow roses, jealousy; white rose buds, girlhood; while a single rose symbolized simplicity. In Greek mythology, the iris, named for the messenger of the gods, represented a message sent. Daisies connoted innocence (left top); tulips, a declaration of love; blue violets, faithfulness, and sweet violets, modesty; mistletoe, a kiss (left center); pansies, thoughts; daffodils, regard; and almond blossoms, hope (left bottom). A single ivy conveyed friendship while a string of ivy signified fidelity.

Not very surprisingly, the rose was one of the most popular flowers as a jewelry subject; it certainly was the favorite of Princess Mathilde, niece of Napoleon I. Even as a young woman, the rose had fond associations for her; admiring young men would press a rose petal to her face to see whether it was possible to distinguish the petal from her cheek.[3] Many years later, in 1854, she purchased a château at Saint-Gratien, located nineteen miles from Paris, where she spent six months of every year tending to her beloved rose garden. That same year she purchased a corsage ornament from the Parisian jeweler, Théodore Fester, located at 2 Rue Vivienne (p. 18). This splendid jewel captures the essence of the rose; a freshly opened flower in the center, surrounded by two buds and several leaves. A short stem completes the perfect life-like form.

The following year, Fester created a corsage spray, reminiscent of seventeenth-century styles, for Empress Eugénie, wife of Emperor Napoleon III, that was set with a multitude of flowers and leaves.[4] That same year, Alfred Bapst created for the empress a currant-leaf parure that was perhaps the grandest of her jewels. It comprised a garland meant to be worn as a necklace, a dress ornament, and a stomacher. The garland consisted of sixteen sections or brooches in the shape of currant leaves, each three-petal section set with a large diamond at its center with aiguillettes set with graduated diamonds representing currants hanging from each leaf (p. 19). This entire ensemble, together with much of the empress' other jewels, was auctioned at the sale of the French crown jewels in 1887. The garland of currant leaves was divided into eight lots that were bought by six different buyers including Bapst, Garrard, and Tiffany & Co.

A necklace with fourteen diamond-set leaves, attributed to Chaumet, is believed to have also been part of the collection of Empress Eugénie (p. 23, bottom). It is made up of different leaves naturalistically depicted as if falling from a tree and may have originally been sewn onto the bodice as a *devant de corsage*.

Seen in brooches as well as necklaces, ivy was a common motif used by designers not only for its symbolic representation but also for its decorative qualities. One of the most impressive was designed by Octave Loeulliard, who was in charge of the Boucheron workshop from 1865 to 1875.[5] His botanical jewelry creations almost seem as if they had been plucked from the plant, even when set with diamonds, as evidenced by the ivy vine necklace (pp. 20–21). Each leaf is attached to a part of the vine that is joined to the next section as it winds around the neck.[6] Boucheron utilized this theme with other plant motifs, such as in a diamond-set necklace ending with a stylized lotus flower terminal after encircling the neck with a simple gold loop (p. 24, left). It was part of their display at the 1889 Exposition Universelle in Paris.

Boucheron also created botanical-inspired jewelry with plique-à-jour, an enameling technique that entails filling open spaces in the metal with translucent enamel which, after several firings, gives the effect of a stained-glass window when held up to the light. The background of a bracelet from this firm was executed in this technique with diamond-set tendrils and flowers providing the decorative design (p. 26).

Top: This gold brooch, probably French, c. 1900, is formed with six tulips with diamonds forming the grass, and pearls the tulip heads. Bottom: An American gold mistletoe brooch set with chalcedony berries, c. 1900, symbolizes a kiss.

Opposite: Made by Theodore Fester in 1854 for Princess Mathilde Bonaparte, a niece of Napoleon, this brooch was designed as a naturalistic rose blossom with diamonds in silver-topped gold. It is said to contain 2,637 diamonds, weighing 136 carats, not counting 860 smaller diamonds. After the death of Princess Mathilde in 1904, Cartier sold the brooch to Mrs. Cornelius Vanderbilt III, "Queen of New York society."

Right: The currant leaf brooch was once part of a garland consisting of sixteen brooches, made by the Parisian jeweler Alfred Bapst in 1855 for Empress Eugénie. In May 1887 it was included in the sale of the French Crown Jewels and was bought by Tiffany & Co. and, later, sold to Mrs. William B. Astor. In 1936 it was given by her grand-daughter-in-law, Mrs. Vincent Astor, to the beloved Metropolitan opera star Lucrezia Bori upon her farewell performance. Upon Mrs. Bori's death in 1960, the currant leaf brooch was bequeathed to the Metropolitan Opera where it is displayed during the opera season.

Jewelry from the nineteenth century was also made with nonprecious gem material such as coral, which enjoyed a resurgence in popularity about every twenty years or so, beginning with the restoration of the French monarchy in the 1840s and, after Napoleon III's unification of Italy in 1860. In the 1840s, coral replaced precious gemstones, as seen on a tiara in which finely carved coral berries "grow" from gold stems with leaves that are colored and textured to suggest the actual plant (p. 14). But it was in the 1860s when coral became available from Naples that this organic substance was incorporated into a variety of jewelry designs either carved in high relief into branches with leaves and flowers in elaborate parures or sculpted as grapes amid gold leaves and vines (p. 29). A few years later, Carlo Giuliano, a jeweler working in London, created a set of flower hair ornaments and a brooch with coral forming the petals and pistils (p. 28).

The last half of the nineteenth century saw a revival in jewelry based on recently unearthed artifacts from antiquity. The Castellani were the foremost exponents of this style, creating diadems, brooches, and necklaces with symbolic botanical motifs. One example is a gold diadem of oak leaves and acorns, known as a civic crown, which they exhibited at the 1862 International Exhibition in London.[7] They also created a bracelet and brooch with millefiori[8] and a diadem of olive leaves.[9] The inspiration for a grapevine necklace made out of gold leaf and purple glass-bead bunches of

grapes necklace (p. 30) came from an Etruscan example, now in the National Museum of Archaeology in Taranto, Italy.[10]

Other exponents of the archeological revival style who made jewelry with botanical motifs were Eugene Fontenay, Jules and Louis Wièse, and Robert Phillips, the latter a London jeweler who, in the 1850s, made reproductions of Etruscan jewelry in the papal collection, which he exhibited at the 1855 Exposition Universelle in Paris. He also designed a necklace with gold ivy-leaf pendants alternating with gold ball pendants strung on a loop-in-loop chain in the antique style (p. 31).

The revival of mosaics became a powerful means for jewelers to display not only their skill at the craft but also the beauty of the gem material they used. The two centers that specialized in mosaics were located in Rome and Florence, with each city producing very different work. In Florence, a technique called either Florentine mosaic or *pietra dura*, was executed by cutting vari-colored hardstones into thin blocks and fitting them together into a bed of black marble to form desired patterns, often sprays of flowers and leaves, especially roses and lilies of the valley (p. 32, right). Alternatively, in the Roman technique of micromosaic, miniature glass tesserae of various colors were carefully placed to compose highly detailed tableaux whose subtle gradations replicated desired tonalities with the fidelity of fine paintings. Notable botanical motifs realized in this technique include medallions with baskets of flowers based on Netherlandish still lifes and a bangle bracelet adorned with grape vines, clusters of roses, and other flowers (both p. 32). The Castellani created just a few examples of micromosaic in floral patterns. One such brooch, donated to the British Museum by Professor and Mrs. Hull Grundy, was inscribed with Greek characters EYTE (translated as "Bravo") surrounded by a wreath of vines with grape bunches and leaves.[11] The firm also created another brooch with micromosaic black-and-white florets (p. 33, right).

Floral jewelry was also decorated with enameling that defined the design as a painting, such as on a pair of reversible cloisonné enameled ear pendants by Alexis Falize where butterflies alight on flowers (p. 34). It was also evident in repetitive decorative patterning as seen on a curling ribbon-style bracelet with forget-me-nots that alternate with textured links (p. 33). However, the most striking examples of enameled floral jewelry were those that closely replicated actual flowers. The manufacturing jewelers in Newark, New Jersey, developed a true specialty in such brooches, creating a variety of flowers that were expertly enameled in graduating shades to capture the essence of the blooms. A good example is the Hedges & Co. demiparure of violets in purple and white tones with a pearl serving as the pistil (p. 37, left). The pansy became a popular flower model for many Newark jewelers as well as retailers such as Tiffany & Co.; Crane & Theurer depicted one in blue and white tones, outlined by gold and set with a diamond at the center (p. 37, top). Whiteside & Blank chose white and pink colors for a flower with thin gold veins on the petals (p. 37, bottom). Krementz & Co., who were credited for revolutionizing the construction of the one-piece collar

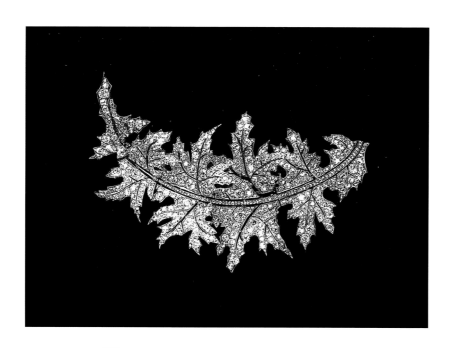

Left: This diamond thistle leaf brooch by Boucheron was made by Octave Loeuillard, one of the house's master jewelers during the late 1800s. It was exhibited at the Exhibition des Arts du Métal at the Union Centrale des Arts Décoratifs in Paris in 1880. Middle: This diamond-set-in-silver-topped-gold leaf brooch was made by Tiffany & Co. in the late 1880s. Bottom: The group of six diamond-set leaves are purported to be by Chaumet and were once part of the collection of Empress Eugénie, wife of Emperor Napoleon III of France. They would either have been mounted onto a necklace or sewn onto a bodice as a *devant de corsage*, c. 1850–75.

Opposite: Several examples of necklaces
by Boucheron date to the 1880s.

Right: A Boucheron diamond-set necklace
features a semi-rigid pavé-set wire that
encircles the neck, ending with an elaborate blossom and leaves which asymmetrically fall down the décolletage, c. 1890.

Below: Boucheron created many examples
of jewelry with plique-à-jour enameling
in the 1870s such as this bracelet that is
overlaid with diamond tendrils and flowers.

Opposite: At the beginning of the 1880s,
the spray began a popular form of jewelry.
Tiffany & Co. created one of silver-topped
gold, diamonds, and conch pearl in the
form of a branch with berries (top). A
French version of the spray is a fuchsia
with enameled flowers, diamond-set
leaves and a single drop pearl (right). This
small diamond-set gold brooch, English
c. 1870, suspends two walnuts made out
of idocrase, a mineral found on Mt.
Vesuvius (bottom). All are superimposed
over Mauboussin drawings from the
same period.

button, made a sweet pea set with a diamond to depict a dew drop, the stone serving as a "sparkle point" (p. 37, right). In the 1890s, interiors were lit by either candles or gas lamps so these little gemstones would twinkle in the flickering light. Adding a small diamond to catch the light was a hallmark of many Newark jewelers.

The enameled flowers from Newark were naturalistically depicted, a characteristic of floral jewelry from the late nineteenth century when jewelers strove to create specimens that looked as though they had been plucked from the stem. This interest in replicating nature was influenced by such artists as Martin Johnson Heade whose hummingbird and orchid studies from the 1860s and 1870s were painted against the backdrop of their Brazilian habitat.[12] He is reputed to have painted the birds and flowers so precisely that, in some respects, he was thought of as much a naturalist as an artist. Darwin, who also knew Heade, wrote about orchids during this time period.[13]

Although there are no extant records to ascertain whether Tiffany & Co.'s chief jewelry designer, Paulding Farnham, knew Heade or had read Darwin's treatises, the orchid brooches he designed for the 1889 Exposition Universelle in Paris are certainly as similar in their attention to naturalistic details as the orchids in Heade's paintings (p. 38 and p. 39, right). These orchids were perfect reproductions of plants that had been shipped to the Tiffany design studio from Guatemala, the Philippines, Columbia, India, Mexico, and Brazil where they were coated with copper to pre-

serve them for study.[14] Farnham's orchids were so lifelike that one reviewer commented, ". . . only actual touch could convince the observer that they were the work of man's hands."[15] In fact, while they were on view at the Tiffany store before they were sent to Paris, George Gould, an avid orchid gardener, purchased several for his collection.[16]

Farnham collaborated for many years with George Frederick Kunz, Tiffany's eminent gemologist, in the selection of unusual gemstones for his jewelry designs. For the 1900 Exposition Universelle in Paris, Farnham created an impressive iris corsage ornament, set with 139 Montana sapphires that Kunz had found in the Yogo Gulch mines in Montana (p. 43, right). These sapphires are a cornflower blue, perfectly suitable for the velvety color gradations of the iris. This notable piece is 9 1/2 inches in length and, although equipped with a pin, it was always intended for exhibition purposes. Purchased by Henry Walters, it is now part of the collection of the Walters Art Museum in Baltimore. Farnham was so pleased with this iris that he had another made with rhodolite garnets, which he presented to his wife, the sculptress Sally Jane Farnham whose *Simon Bolivar* stands in Central Park, New York (p. 43, left).

Although there are no precise records to substantiate many of the jewels that Farnham designed, the Tiffany orchid made with American freshwater pearls is characteristic of jewelry that he designed in collaboration with Kunz (p. 40, right). In Kunz's, *The Book of the Pearl*, published in 1908, there is a plate illustrating five brooches made out of petal, dog-tooth, and wing pearls that

Left: This demiparure consisting of a gold brooch and matching earrings in the form of coral grape clusters dates from the 1860s and was part of the collection of the American heiress Doris Duke. The grape was a popular symbol in the nineteenth century, representing fecundity, plenty, and an expanding nation. Doris Duke Charitable Foundation. Below: This group of American vari-colored gold flowers and leaves set with diamonds and pearls dates to the 1880s.

were probably designed by Farnham.[17] The variety of different freshwater pearls of the dog-tooth, wing, and baroque type on this orchid brooch would point to a Farnham design.

Another important American maker, Marcus & Co., whose jewelry rivaled that of Tiffany & Co., created a realistic chrysanthemum brooch out of dog-tooth pearls that were most likely found in the Pecatonica River, a tributary to the Mississippi River (p. 40, left). The petals radiate outward from a central point just as they do in real flowers. The two leaves emerging from the short stem are set with diamonds. With its use of pearls and diamonds, this brooch was designed in the manner of Edwardian jewelry from the turn of the century when the all-white look was popular.

Botanically inspired jewelry of the nineteenth century ran the gamut from diamond-set sprays to be worn pinned to shoulders or bodices to full-colored enameled, colored gemstone, or freshwater pearl flowers that seemed almost real. A major emphasis was to capture nature's beauty, often with impressive realism. Imaginative designers created a host of styles and variations that appealed to each and every taste for the beautiful and left a rich legacy for us to admire and enjoy today.

This necklace by Castellani, c. 1870 is designed in the archaeological revival style as a woven chain supporting gold vine leaves that alternate with purple paste bead bunches of grapes.

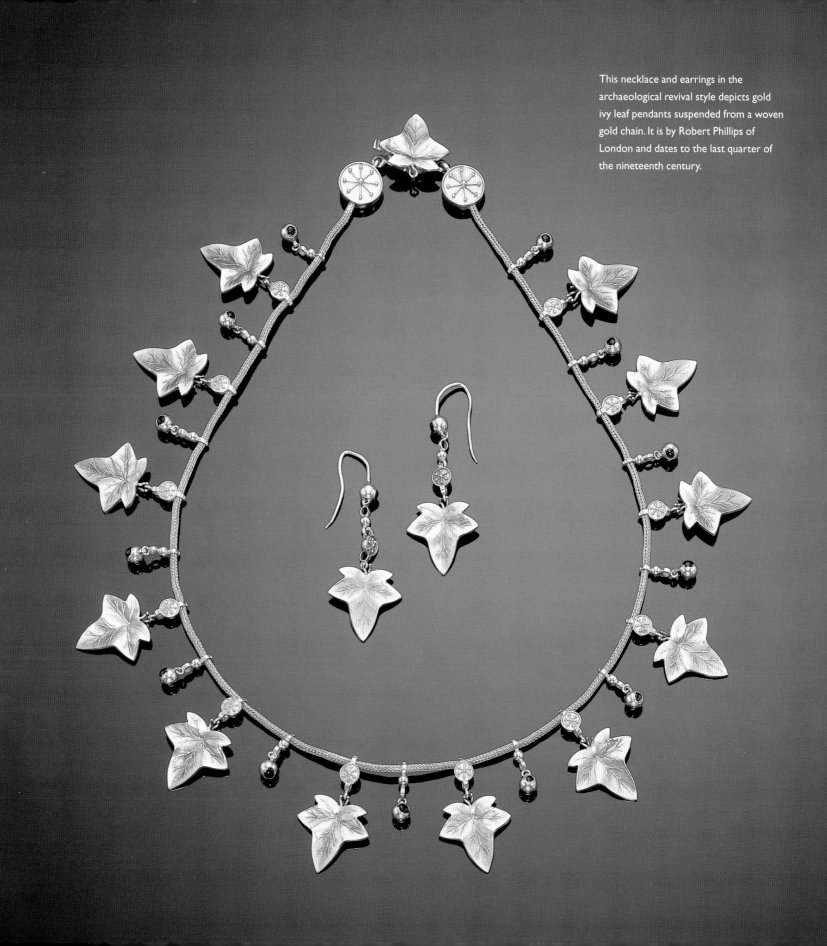

This necklace and earrings in the archaeological revival style depicts gold ivy leaf pendants suspended from a woven gold chain. It is by Robert Phillips of London and dates to the last quarter of the nineteenth century.

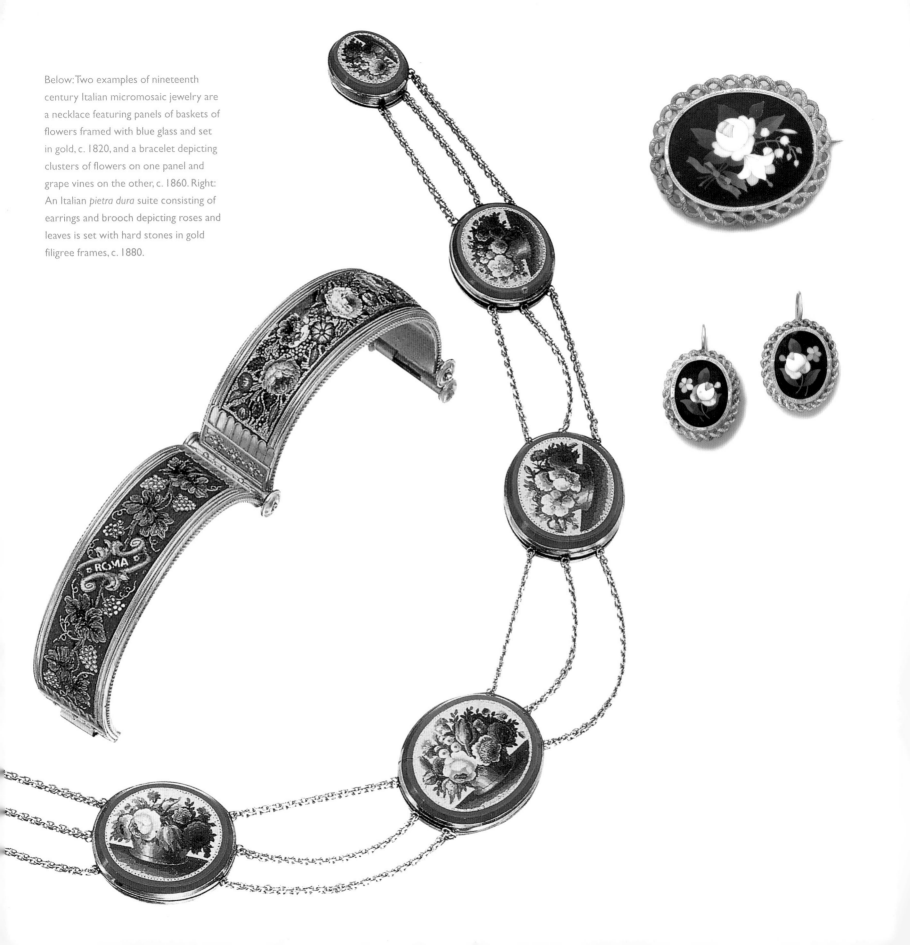

Below: Two examples of nineteenth century Italian micromosaic jewelry are a necklace featuring panels of baskets of flowers framed with blue glass and set in gold, c. 1820, and a bracelet depicting clusters of flowers on one panel and grape vines on the other, c. 1860. Right: An Italian *pietra dura* suite consisting of earrings and brooch depicting roses and leaves is set with hard stones in gold filigree frames, c. 1880.

Left: A revivalist gold and micromosaic pendant brooch from the last quarter of the nineteenth century is decorated with a bouquet of flowers on the amphora pendant and a vine with flowers on the supporting bar. Below top: A gold and micromosaic pin by Castellani dates to c. 1870. Bottom: This gold and diamond bracelet, decorated with enameled forget-me-nots, dates to the last quarter of the nineteenth century.

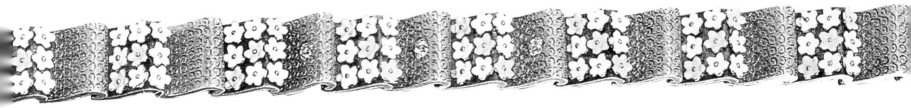

Right: The Whiteland's May Queen's Cross in the form of a spray of hawthorn flowers and leaves was designed by Arthur Severn. It is engraved on the reverse "Ruskin Cross presented to E. Hand. May 1st 1893."
Bottom: A pair of earrings by Alexis Falize is decorated with cloisonné enamels in the Japanesque taste, c. 1870.

Three pairs of pendant earrings from the late nineteenth century include bunches of grapes hanging from the vine, English, c. 1880 (right); enameled vignettes of colorful flowers, French, 1870s (bottom); and Etruscan revival stylized daisies with granulation, English, c. 1880 (left).

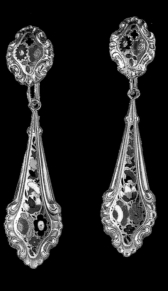

Opposite: The American jeweler Theodore B. Starr created an impressive gold, enamel, and gem-set necklace, c. 1895.

Right: This group of enamel and gem-set flower jewelry dating from 1895 to 1900 was made in the manufacturing center of Newark, New Jersey including clockwise from right to left: a pansy by Crane & Theurer, a sweet pea by Krementz & Co., a pink flower by Whiteside & Blank, and a suite of violets by Hedges & Co.

Opposite: Four diamond-and-gem-set enameled orchid brooches were designed by Paulding Farnham for Tiffany & Co., examples of which were included in the 1889 Exposition Universelle in Paris.

Right: This diamond and enameled orchid brooch is attributed to Henri Vever, c. 1900. Lower right: This is another enameled orchid designed by Paulding Farnham for Tiffany & Co. Below: Gold and enamel cufflinks by Tiffany & Co., c. 1890–5, depict orchids.

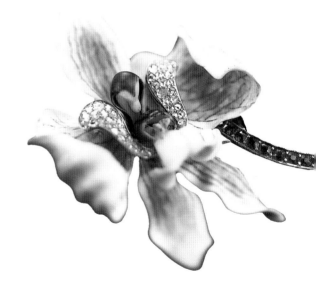

Left: A chrysanthemum blossom by Marcus & Co., c. 1900, is formed of dog-tooth pearls and mounted on a curved stem with diamond-set gold and platinum leaves. The gold on the reverse of the flower head is realistically engraved to resemble the actual specimen. Bottom: Dog-tooth, wing, and baroque freshwater pearls form the petals of this orchid brooch by Tiffany & Co., c. 1900, set with a diamond at the center.

A species of *Hoya* by Tiffany & Co. c.1890 is made with pink enameled flowers with diamond pistils and diamond-set leaves (left). A diamond, gold, and platinum mignonette with enameled flowers is similar to an example Tiffany & Co exhibited at the 1889 Exposition Universelle in Paris (right). Both flowers were designed by Paulding Farnham.

This large, three-dimensional tulip brooch dates from the late 1800s and was made by the Parisian atelier Baugrand in sapphires, rubies, emeralds, and diamonds set in gold.

Opposite right: The iris brooch is set with 139 Montana sapphires, demantoid garnets, topaz, and diamonds. It was designed by Paulding Farnham for Tiffany & Co's exhibit at the 1900 Exposition Universelle in Paris and was later purchased by railroad magnate and art collector Henry Walters. The Walters Art Museum, Baltimore. Opposite left: About the same time that Farnham designed the iris brooch, he created a smaller version with rhodolite garnets, demantoid garnets, and diamonds set in gold, which he presented to his wife, the sculptor Sally James Farnham.

The poppy flowers and leaves on this *plaque de cou* by Louis Aucoc, c. 1900, are rendered in plique-à-jour enameling; the flowers have diamond pistils. Diamonds set in platinum depict a background of rippling water. The Newark Museum.

CHAPTER TWO

The Early Twentieth Century

Two Parallel Movements: Art Nouveau and Edwardian

By the end of the nineteenth century, jewelry design had evolved into two entirely different styles, both employing imaginative botanical themes. One followed in the wake of Victorian design, using traditional metals and gemstones while the other veered off onto an artistic path, utilizing strikingly new materials and techniques. Jewelry from these two divergent directions appealed to very different clienteles: the wealthy sophisticate who still wanted diamond-set jewelry, or the avant-garde who clamored after the new and unusual. The former is a style that has come to be known as Edwardian, named after King Edward VII who reigned from 1901 to 1910, and the latter, Art Nouveau, which took its name from Siegfried Bing's Parisian L'Art Nouveau gallery, which opened on December 26, 1895. Bing showcased what he perceived as "the new art" in painting, sculpture, the decorative arts, and jewelry; René Lalique was among the first group of jewelers that he presented.

The term "Art Nouveau" has come to define the period from 1895 to about 1910, when a select number of jewelers worked in a style radically different from anything that had been done before. It featured free-flowing, curving lines with asymmetrical naturalistic motifs. Horn and ivory were worked into wondrous shapes, metals were made to look like organic substances, and gemstones were set to appear as if they were growing out of the metal. Enameling, which had been popular in the latter quarter of the nineteenth century, not only added color to a piece of jewelry but, with the further development of plique-à-jour, its see-through appearance replaced large sections of metal, creating a gossamer look. But what really made Art Nouveau revolutionary was design that took jewelry from pure ornament enhancing the wearer, to an art form—nowhere is this more evident than in jewelry with botanical imagery.

Just as in the nineteenth century, when books and articles guided designers toward new ways of interpreting plant life into jewelry design, Art Nouveau designers turned to illustrated books for inspiration. A notable source was *La Plante et ses applications ornamentales*, edited by the Swiss artist Eugène Grasset and published in monthly installments from 1896 to 1900. Graphic artist Alphonse Mucha's *Documents décoratifs* also illustrated metalwork and jewelry modeled after plants. But it was perhaps Christopher Dresser's *Unity in Variety* from 1859 that most influenced Art Nouveau designers. His illustrations served as precursors to Art Nouveau imagery with an emphasis on the growth of plants.[1]

Art Nouveau redefined the choice of plants as models. Instead of rendering the plant at its most opportune moment—a perfect specimen in full bloom—jewelry designers portrayed the growth cycle of a flower from bud to decay, capturing a single flower with petals about to open, others fully open, and some closed. Their depiction suggested reality. Preferred flowers included hothouse varieties as well as wild flowers. Vivienne Becker in *Art Nouveau Jewelry* aptly describes their characteristics, ". . . the rare orchid, languid lilies, erect sunflowers, shaggy carnations, or the simple field flowers, the heavy umbellifers, the poppy with its scarlet limp petals, the mistletoe, or honesty with its flat, translucent seed pods."[2] There was a feeling of movement, of energy within the plant. They were no longer just ornamental blooms but flowers that pulsated with life.

In some respects, this approach to nature was an outgrowth of Japonism, of looking at nature in its natural state. Lucien Gaillard, who was captivated by the charm of Japanese works as early as 1878,[3] created jewelry with flowers and leaves captured in the cycle of life, with leaves partially eaten by insects.[4] From Japonism he also learned how to portray nature without extraneous details, as on a bracelet with a continuous frieze of branches with dogwood blossoms that stretch across eight panels, which calls to mind Japanese screens (opposite, top).

Gaillard was a skilled practitioner in metallurgy as well as in working with other unusual materials such as ivory, a material that several jewelers used to advantage during the Art Nouveau period. He carved it into sheaves of wheat framed with gold mounts to protect the edges on a necklace that he exhibited at the 1907 La Société des Artistes Français (p. 48). But it was René Lalique, the undisputed leader of Art Nouveau jewelry, who shaped ivory into sculptural, almost ethereal forms, seeming to defy their limitations. His first piece in this material was a bracelet made with a slice of ivory decorated with silver ornaments.[5] But the truly spectacular jewels that he created out of ivory were orchids; their petals carved so thinly that it seems as if the flower had just been plucked from the stem. The lateral petals on the cattleya orchid tiara are larger than the sepals and the tubular labellum has a projecting lower lip, giving it an almost surreal, erotic effect (p. 51).[6]

Top: An articulated bracelet by Lucien Gaillard, c. 1900, is decorated with enamel dogwood blossoms and branches against a pale green plique-à-jour enamel background. Bottom: This pine branches bracelet in gold, plique à jour enamel and tourmalines was made by René Lalique, c. 1900.

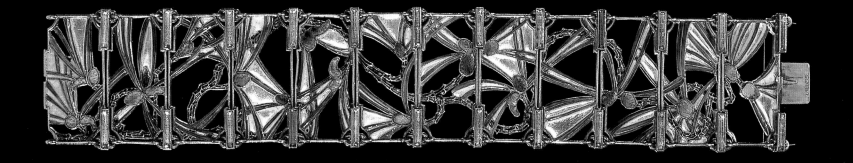

Horn, another nontraditional jewelry substance used in simple combs and other small decorative objects, became a key component of impressive Art Nouveau creations. It could be heated, and then worked into desirable shapes such as hazelnut leaves on a tiara (p. 54) or a single leaf on a comb, both by Lalique (p. 55). Lalique frequently used the hazelnut in jewelry,[7] probably because its serrated leaves lent attractive contrast to the bracts, leaf-like parts holding the woody nuts, which were glass on the tiara and gold on the comb.

Lalique exhibited a hazelnut necklace at the 1900 Exposition Universelle in Paris,[8] which was probably the design source for the brooch created by the New York jeweler Marcus & Co. (p. 54). Instead of horn, the leaves on this brooch are crafted with plique-à-jour enameling and the green translucent coloring is picked up in the bracts, while the nuts are in pink shades of translucent enamel. The leaves on this brooch are three-dimensional with realistic curling edges; it resembles the actual plant in a refined and beautiful way.

Landscapes and seasons were also themes in Art Nouveau jewelry; the passage of time reflected Japonism. Autumn with its mellow colors symbolized the fading century. Lalique depicted the coldness of winter via snow-covered firs with a bluish tinge of icy stillness (p. 53). Water often featured in landscapes. On a *plaque de cou*, Louis Aucoc captured just a snapshot of a scene with a mass of three-dimensional poppy flowers growing in different directions against a background of rippling water, set with diamonds to show the glint from the sun (p. 44). Although a piece of jewelry, it is created in the tradition of landscape paintings.

Lalique also perfected the use of glass in his botanical jewelry. In the early 1890s, he began experimenting with different techniques at his studio, exhibiting his first glass objects at the 1895 Salon. By 1900, he was creating pieces of meticulous detail and craftsmanship, such as a pendant necklace of patinated glass poppies (p. 56), a bracelet with molded glass speedwells (p. 58), and a brooch with blackberries (p. 59).

Blackberries were not a plant motif that appealed to most designers; however, like Lalique, Louis Comfort Tiffany preferred the less mundane in his botanical creations, exhibiting jewelry in the 1904 Louisiana Purchase Exposition in St. Louis[9] derived from ". . . species commonly met in the fields or woods, or yet along country roads: among them being the clover, the wild carrot, the bittersweet, the blackberry, the mountain ash, and the spirea."[10] Tiffany's muse was nature and this theme is pervasive in every area of his oeuvre from decorative art objects including glass, ceramics, enamels, and leaded glass lamps to stained-glass windows, each enriched with colors true to the original specimen.

Tiffany turned to the grapevine motif again and again, beginning with a necklace he designed for the St. Louis fair set with black opals simulating grapes amid enameled leaves.[11] A few years later, after 1907 when his jewelry was made at Tiffany & Co., he created a necklace with interlocking links shaped to resemble gnarled vines to which are attached gold grape leaves with veins chased

Opposite: A necklace by Lucien Gaillard depicts wheat sheaves in carved ivory mounted into gold. It was exhibited at the Société des Artistes Français in 1907 and won the gold medal for design.

on both sides of each leaf, and beads of nephrite forming bunches of grapes (p. 62). A brooch continues the grape subject with a compact massing of cabochon tourmalines and faceted sapphires to simulate grapes amid leaves partially eaten by insects (p. 61, left), a theme borrowed from Japanese art.

Supporting the popularity of the grape motif in the first two decades of the twentieth century, both Marcus & Co. and Van Cleef & Arpels used natural pearls for grapes. The leaves on the former are plique-à-jour enameling (p. 63, center); on the latter they are set with diamonds (p. 63, right). The Van Cleef & Arpels brooch is an example of the Edwardian style, which Hans Nadelhoffer describes in *Cartier Jewelers Extraordinary* as "the garland style."[12] Characterized by graceful, elegant lines, this style was not a new design aesthetic but rather a derivative of the Louis XVI style that had been revitalized by Empress Eugénie in the 1850s when she had the French crown jewels remade in the likeness of Marie Antoinette's jewelry.

The Edwardian style would not have been feasible without the introduction of platinum into jewelry fabrication. Not only did the untarnishable whiteness of this metal complement diamonds but its great strength also meant that it took less material to hold stones in place, thus enabling settings to become so dainty as to be hardly visible from the front. As a result of this new technical freedom of form, the Edwardian or garland style, in spite of its eighteenth-century origins, came to be seen as a new design aesthetic that offered an alternative to Art Nouveau. Swags and festooned garlands embellished with fruits and flowers, grape bunches, ferns, thistles, lilies, eglantines, laurel leaves, and baskets of flowers became de rigueur in fashionable jewelry.

Among the many jewelers in the first two decades of the twentieth century, Cartier stood at the forefront, creating well-designed jewelry that accessorized the tight-fitting fashion of the day. The new "S"-shape silhouette based on the new Gibson girl ideal demanded jewels that were sewn into bodices, draped around necks, or suspended from shoulders. Examples of Cartier's offerings for the new fashion include a special pair of fern-spray brooches that could be worn in many different ways—as brooches or, when joined together, as a corsage ornament, or draped on the shoulder (p. 65). With special fittings, it also became a diadem or a necklace. The lily and eglantine corsage ornament is another tour de force of Cartier design (p. 64). Articulated branches of lilies that cross at the base are decorated with garlands of eglantines that soften the design. The entire ensemble gives the effect of a festoon or half of a wreath.

The laurel leaf was perhaps the most prevalent botanical image during this period, appearing on every type of jewelry. In Greek mythology, the laurel tree was sacred to Apollo and expressive of victory; laurel leaves, woven into festive garlands and crowns, were presented to victors at athletic competitions as well as given to poets and artists as recognition of their accomplishments. This connotation prevailed into the twentieth century with the image becoming a natural device for

Below: A *plaque de cou* with seed pearl necklace by Lucien Gaillard, c. 1900, is designed with a central enameled plaque depicting chrysanthemums. The two flowers have opal centers surrounded by petals in rose-beige enamel and leaves in green enamel. It was exhibited in the 1903 Paris Salon.

Opposite: The Winter Landscape pendant by René Lalique, c. 1899–1900, portrays a winter scene with a molded intaglio glass panel with tree trunks framed by a snowy evergreen tree in white opaque enamel on the gold mounting. It is set with imitation glass marquise-cut stones and there is a natural gray pearl suspended from a branch.

adorning tiaras and diadems such as the example by Boucheron with rays of diamond-set laurel leaves and an unmarked diadem with wreaths of diamond-set laurel leaves (both p. 67).

During the Edwardian era, botanical images were also rendered in whimsical jewelry such as a mother-of-pearl pea pod with pearls forming the peas (p. 60) or a pair of thistle brooches (p. 66). Carl Fabergé, best known for his workshop that produced elaborate eggs for the Russian tsar and his family, produced jewelry with imaginative imagery such as a flower, set with an aquamarine, that was inspired by Catherine the Great's jewelry (p. 66).[13] Baskets of flowers, which had been seen in jewelry from the late eighteenth century, once again became a favored motif. In the mid teens, Cartier made a basket with pearl and diamond-set flowers and leaves and hexagonally cut diamonds forming the buds, presaging by several years the geometric cuts seen later in Art Deco jewelry (p. 69, top).

Another piece that looks to the next decade is a bracelet by the Paris house of Lacloche Frères, who became known for the elegant jewelry they offered during the first three decades of the twentieth century. Instead of setting diamonds into traditional platinum mountings arranged into recognizable designs or patterns, the stones in this bracelet are mounted onto a delicate web-like structure, resembling a petit point of rose blossoms, leaves, and stems with thorns that appear as if "stitched" onto the metal (p. 66). The arrangement of the flowers bears affinities to elements on the decorative arts and tapestries of the French interior designers, Süe et Mare.

The period from the late nineteenth century to the second decade of the twentieth century was a time of elegance as well as a time of revolutionary design in jewelry, when botanical motifs evolved from purely decorative ornamentation to works of art. The enormous impact of World War I resulted in the final denouement of the Edwardian and Art Nouveau eras. It was a time of rethinking, of casting off styles based on curvilinear shapes or on the eighteenth century. What took its place was radically different, a new vernacular based on rectilinear design.

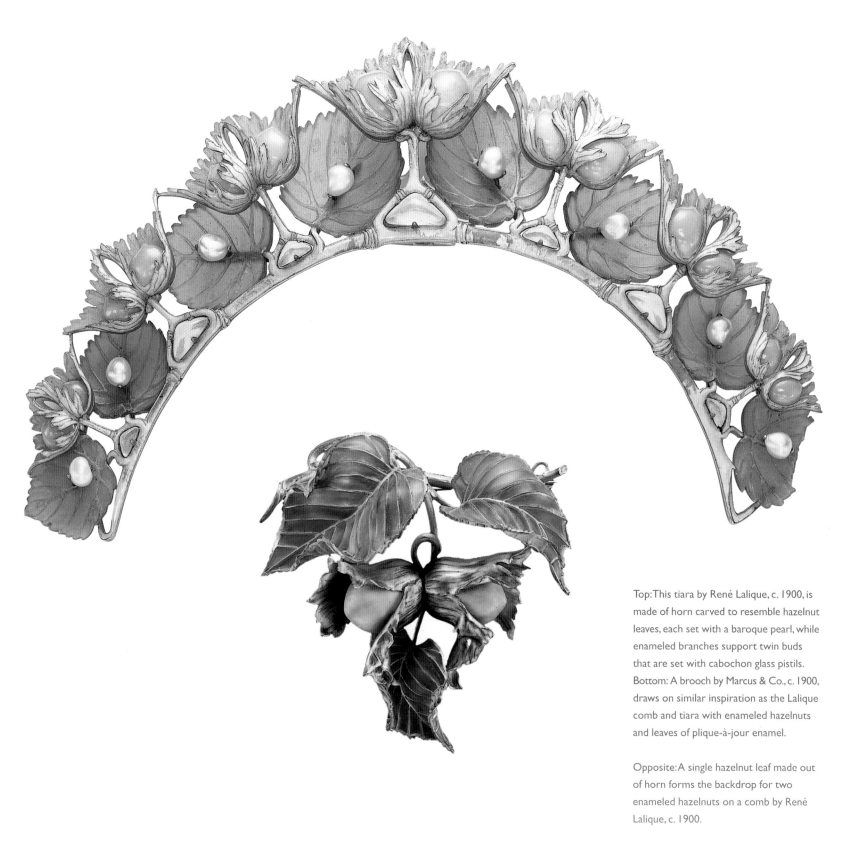

Top: This tiara by René Lalique, c. 1900, is made of horn carved to resemble hazelnut leaves, each set with a baroque pearl, while enameled branches support twin buds that are set with cabochon glass pistils. Bottom: A brooch by Marcus & Co., c. 1900, draws on similar inspiration as the Lalique comb and tiara with enameled hazelnuts and leaves of plique-à-jour enamel.

Opposite: A single hazelnut leaf made out of horn forms the backdrop for two enameled hazelnuts on a comb by René Lalique, c. 1900.

Below: A large gold and plique-à-jour enamel poppy brooch is set with diamond accents, French, c. 1900. Right: René Lalique simulated a naturalistic anemone plant in this necklace using painted glass flowers, diamond-set gold stems, and enameled leaves, c. 1900–3. Toledo Museum of Art.

René Lalique created this naturalistically
designed pussy-willow diadem out of
horn, mother-of-pearl, enamel, and topaz
around 1903.

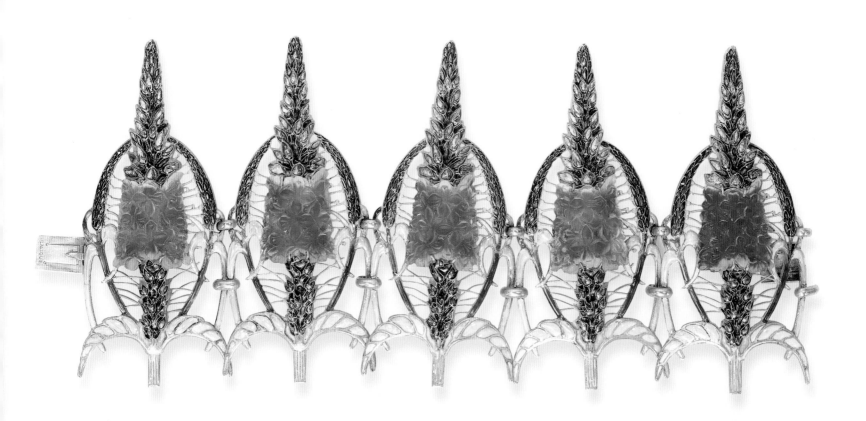

Opposite: This bracelet by René Lalique, c. 1900, is composed of five purple-backed molded glass speedwell blossoms with champlevé enamel stems and with open-work blue and green enamel surround.

Left: A pendant by René Lalique, c. 1900, is made in the form of blackberries in opalescent molded glass with leaves of green plique-à-jour enamel. Bottom: Georges Fouquet designed this bandeau, c. 1910, with panels of green plique-à-jour enamel clover leaves amid diamonds intersected with rectangular-cut aquamarines.

Left: This brooch from the Edwardian period, c. 1910, was created as a pea pod made of pearls and mother-of-pearl framed in platinum-set diamonds, with leaves of emeralds set in gold, and a stem of diamonds set into platinum. Below: This 33 ½-inch chain and lorgnette was designed by René Lalique around 1900. The chain contains jade beads, openwork plaques of gold with white enamel vines, and plique-à-jour enamel leaves surrounding flowers set with diamonds. The lorgnette is in the same material. The Metropolitan Museum of Art, New York.

Opposite top: This necklace, in mother-of-pearl and freshwater American pearls, depicting a stylized vine, is by the Kalo Shop of Chicago and is representative of the American arts and crafts movement, c. 1910–15. Opposite right: A brooch by Georges Fouquet, c. 1900, is designed with a baroque pearl entwined by plique-à-jour enamel leaves and accented with a cabochon sapphire. Opposite left: This brooch with cabochon green tourmalines accented with Montana sapphires amid gold leaves was designed by Louis Comfort Tiffany, c. 1915–20, and made by Tiffany & Co. Louis C. Tiffany Garden Museum, Japan.

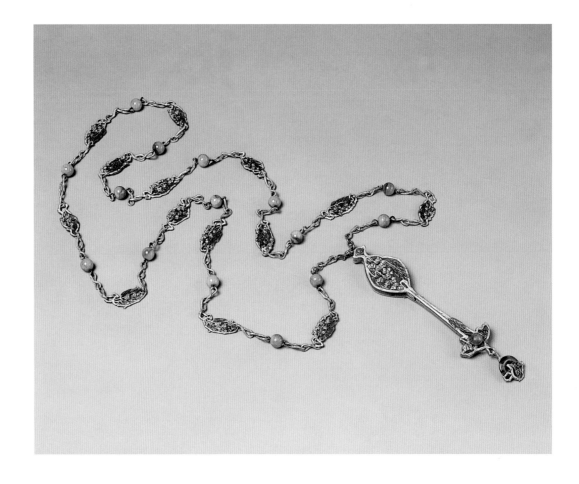

Opposite: On this necklace designed by Louis Comfort Tiffany grape clusters of nephrites set amid gold leaves hang from interlocking links of gold resembling grapevines, Tiffany & Co., c. 1912. Toledo Museum of Art.

Right: Three grape-vine brooches exemplify the Art Nouveau and Edwardian movements. An Art Nouveau example by Marcus & Co., c. 1900, is made with baroque pearl grapes and plique-à-jour enamel leaves highlighted by diamond set veins (Top). The Toledo Museum of Art. Both characteristic of the Edwardian style, the Van Cleef & Arpels grape cluster has stems and leaves in platinum set with diamonds and white natural pearls, c. 1915 (right), while multicolored pearls make up the grape cluster on another brooch, c. 1910 (bottom).

Opposite: Cartier made this tiara that could be converted into a corsage brooch on a necklace. It depicts two sprays of lilies intertwined with garlands of eglantine. Made in platinum set with diamonds in 1906, its inspiration almost certainly derives from the idea of crossed sprays of laurel leaves, a motif present during the eighteenth century.

Right: Another convertible jewel from Cartier, these two fern spray brooches are not only articulated, but can be worn together as a *devant de corsage*, a diadem, or a necklace. By Charpentier for Cartier Paris for stock, in 1903, they are made of diamonds in open-back platinum mille-grain settings.

Far right: These two thistle brooches, c. 1915, are in millegrain platinum set with rose-cut diamonds. Right: This silver-topped gold diamond-set brooch by Carl Fabergé, c. 1908, is with an aquamarine as the flower head. Below: This pierced platinum and diamond bracelet of roses by Lacloche Frères, French, c. 1915 is designed to resemble petit point.

Opposite top: This tiara, made by Boucheron in 1909, depicts branches of laurel leaves made with rose-cut diamonds set in platinum and terminating with pearls. Opposite bottom: A diadem with wreaths of diamond-set laurel leaves dates to c. 1905.

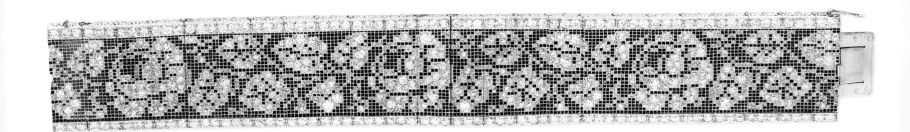

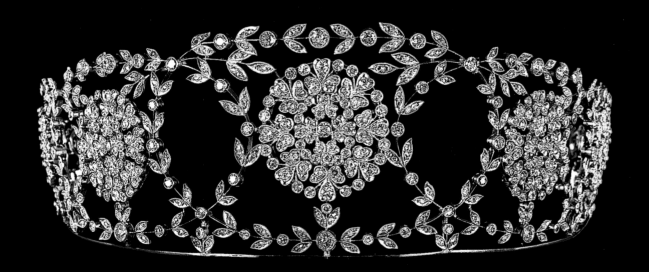

Below: The gold laurel leaves and berries tiara is in the shape of a wreath. It is inscribed: "To Vira Boarman Whitehouse from the women of New York State whom she led to victory, November 1917." It was presented to Ms. Whitehouse in recognition of her leadership as the chairman of the New York Woman Suffrage Party and the victory of the movement in the New York State Elections in 1917.

Opposite right: The design of this flower basket brooch from the Cartier archives dates from 1912, foreshadowing the introduction of color and geometric lines into jewelry design. Opposite top: This diamond and pearl brooch from 1918 is an example of the later asymmetrical garland style after Cartier opened in New York. Opposite bottom: This diamond and sapphire brooch by Cartier, Paris, 1906, is called a twin circle brooch, as it resembles two interlocked circles.

This brooch by Vever features a carved amethyst flower with an emerald center on a pavé diamond background bordered on two sides by amber columns adorned with black enamel trim and natural pearls, c. 1925.

CHAPTER THREE

The Twenties

Exoticism Meets Modernism to Create Art Deco

In the early nineteen hundreds, several factors and events triggered a dramatic shift in the dominant design aesthetic for jewelry. New art movements such as cubism and futurism created a new vernacular for art. Serge Diaghilev's performances of the Ballets Russes in Paris in 1909 and in the United States in 1916 with its introduction of bright colors as well as the Paris Opera Chinese Ball in 1923 contributed to an interest in the exotic Orient while the opening of Tutankhamen's tomb in 1922 inspired Egyptian motifs. All of these initiated new concepts in jewelry, both in the inspiration and execution.

Up until the Art Deco period, jewelry with botanical motifs was guided by the desire to emulate the beauty of actual specimens from nature's seemingly infinite variety, often in three-dimensional glory. In contrast, the design aesthetic of this period endeavored to abstract nature's beauty into stylized forms composed of simple, geometrical, largely rectilinear shapes. By and large, the fruits and vegetables that had provided attractive models for jewelry design largely disappeared and it was the flower in its many renditions that held sway in the 1920s, most likely because of its adaptability to the new design idiom.

The Art Deco period in jewelry design commenced in the teens and was fully developed by 1920, when geometrical configurations became an established part of the design repertoire. Flowers and plants that had been three-dimensional, became decisively two-dimensional and, more notably, the white look of Edwardian jewelry of the previous decade was completely replaced with a vibrant palette of colors, influenced by the emerging art movements.

As the principal elements in Art Deco jewelry design became simple geometric forms—such as squares, rectangles, circles, and triangles—with flowers and plants rendered in stylized combinations of these, design

Right: This platinum, diamond, carved moonstone, cabochon sapphire, and black enamel stylized flower pin centering a kunzite by Mauboussin was exhibited at the 1925 Paris Salon for Decorative Arts. Bottom right: This bar brooch with a carved carnelian flower surrounded by enameled leaves on gold was made by Raymond Templier, c. 1923 Below: This pansy by the Philadelphia company J. E. Caldwell was fashioned out of a carved black opal with diamond center and stem, c. 1920. Black opal, the most rare and desirable of opals, contains a predominantly dark background which shows off the vibrant mix of surface colors.

became supreme. It was all about the linear treatment of a flower or leaf that could still be recognized and enjoyed as such even if not looking quite as they grew in the garden. The new designs were adorned with the usual gemstones and precious stones. In addition, turquoise, tourmaline, onyx, aquamarine, rock crystal, carnelian, coral, and amethyst were either added for contrast or became the material from which flowers were sculpted. The more unusual the stone, the more desirable it became for crafting botanical images.

Vever Frères carved a rose, the perennial favorite of all flowers, out of amethyst (p. 70) and Raymond Templier did so with carnelian (opposite, bottom). In a veritable tour de force, J. E. Caldwell, a Philadelphia jeweler, sculpted a pansy from a single black opal (opposite, left).[1] Mauboussin created a highly stylized flower out of carved moonstone set with a large kunzite in the center (opposite, top), but it was their use of colored gemstones arranged in interesting patterns that made this firm's jewelry so unique. Mauboussin designers regarded gemstones as their artist's palette, creating play of color as well as strong design. On one lapel watch, geometrically shaped turquoise forms stylized flowers, each set with a sapphire, the bunch arranged in a rock-crystal basket (p. 74, left). Either with gemstones shaped into softened contours, or engraved to form leaves and flowers, the floral basket image was a trademark of the company during the Art Deco period (p. 75).

A customary way of depicting flowers during the 1920s was to present them two-dimensionally, almost as if the blooms were pressed flat. In the bracelet by Marzo, a Parisian designer whose salon was located on the fashionable rue de la Paix, stylized roses resemble floral patterns on textiles (p. 81, top). Boucheron created a spectacular necklace shaped like a trellis with blossoming roses with stylized flowers created in a manner similar to rose decorations by designers in the Glasgow School, especially those by Charles Rennie Mackintosh for the Willow Tea-Rooms (p. 80).[2] The roses on the necklace are grouped into three sections, each one made of domed calibré-cut rubies with a calibré-cut emerald leaf at the bottom of the flower. This necklace was exhibited in the firm's display at the 1925 Exposition Internationale des Arts Décoratifs et Industriels Modernes in Paris.

Below: Cartier created this pictorial bracelet of apple blossoms in cabochon rubies and emeralds with onyx branches on a diamond-set background, c. 1925.

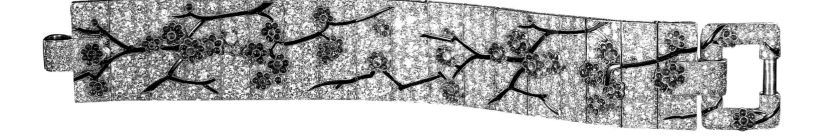

Right: This diamond bracelet by Cartier, New York from 1926 features a crystal compote filled with fruit of ruby beads and is accented with black enamel. Bottom right: A Chinese-inspired brooch by Cartier, New York from 1927 depicts leaf-shape engraved rubies with diamonds and onyx beads set in platinum filling an engraved lapis lazuli vase. Below: This fob watch by Mauboussin, c. 1928, depicts stylized flowers in jade with sapphire and black enamel accents cascading out of a crystal vase.

Opposite: This flower basket brooch and design drawings by Mauboussin date to 1928. The basket on the brooch is made in platinum, diamonds and black enamel with flowers of buff-cut rubies, emeralds, sapphires, amethysts, and onyx. The drawing on the top left is by Cartier.

Right: This rectilinear flower-pot brooch by Tiffany & Co. is set with diamonds, engraved emeralds, and cabochon emeralds, c. 1925. Below top: This rock crystal, diamond, enamel, and emerald brooch with a foliate mount was made by an unknown French maker, c. 1925. Below bottom: A rock crystal, diamond, amethyst, and emerald brooch in the Indian style by Mauboussin, c. 1925, features a vine with leaves of buff-cut emeralds.

Gemstones were used as the base onto which flattened flowers and leaves were affixed. On a Boucheron bracelet, blue enameled flowers with black enameled leaves are applied to jasper panels, with each panel divided into three sections; the tableau reminiscent of Japanese screens (p. 83, bottom). Ernst Paltscho, from Vienna, created a bracelet with blossoms, each with a different gemstone, that are fastened onto a lapis lazuli background (p. 83, center).

The flat, flexible bracelet became the most pervasive piece of jewelry during the Art Deco period and was made by every jeweler. The typical Art Deco dress was sleeveless, which allowed the jewelry designer free rein to create artistic floral designs to decorate the wrist. Because bracelets were narrow, four or five could be worn together on the wrist. By the end of the decade, they became wider but continued to be worn in multiples. The flat, articulated links on these bracelets provided a perfect canvas upon which to draw imaginative designs, some with stylized flowers, others more naturalistic. On a three-panel, flexible example with flowers in buff-top gemstones, Mauboussin chose sapphires for the petals, rubies and purple sapphires for the center of each flower, and emeralds for leaves (p. 79, third down). Because of the almost flat appearance, buff-top cut stones, a type of cabochon cut with the top cut off and slightly rounded at the edges, were perfect for Art Deco jewelry. Janesich, another Parisian designer on the rue de la Paix, created a bracelet in the Oriental taste with a repetitive pattern of chrysanthemums made out of buff-top sapphires on black onyx stems (p. 79, top). Although conceived and executed in an Art Deco manner, the flowers are rendered naturalistically with petals shaped to simulate those on an actual plant.

After the Paris Opera Chinese Ball in 1923, Orientalizing motifs became prevalent on Western jewelry. The naturalistic pattern that appeared most often was based on the continuous-stem principle—where branches reach out to embrace flowers—evident on Chinese enamelware and ceramics. A Cartier bracelet exemplifies the translation of this Oriental motif into a new stylized and geometric Western idiom with apple blossoms arranged in an asymmetrical pattern (p. 73).

After 1925, bracelets became wider, providing a larger surface for designers to make original designs. The extra width enabled the Parisian jewelers Rubel Frères, to accommodate a stylized garden on a bracelet. Evenly spaced pierced flower heads, each set with a pear-shape diamond pistil and a calibré-cut onyx stem, make up the lower part of the composition while colorful ruby flowers peek over the horizon (p. 79, second down).

As an alternative to bracelets with recurring motifs, Tiffany & Co. offered an imaginative design by synthesizing the rectilinear aspect of Art Deco with flowing lines, resulting in a bracelet that is more about art than about a wearable piece of jewelry. It is designed with a rose growing out of a flower pot with a diamond set into a dark blue sky above (p. 78). The design is carefully arranged with the sinuous stem leading the eye to the full bloom while also serving to soften the rectilinear design. When laid flat, the entire rose is visible but, when strapped to the wrist, only parts of it are seen and must be turned for the full design to be viewed.

But it was Cartier who set the standard for design during the Art Deco period, creating jewelry with a flair for the dramatic but always with understated elegance. These pieces have become signature designs of the era. Every type of jewelry they made was treated with attention to detail, from small pieces such as a sureté pin that is composed of overlapping carved turquoise and diamond leaves (p. 82, right) to a bracelet with ruby beads simulating fruit in a rock-crystal basket (p. 74).

The truly remarkable botanical jewelry that Cartier created at this time were bracelets, necklaces, watches, brooches, earrings, cliquet pins, and handbag mountings of multigemstone assembly of engraved rubies, sapphires, and emeralds. When the style was first introduced, it was referred to as "leaf work," but because of its colorful resemblance to floral and fruit baskets, it has come to be known as "Tutti Frutti" or "fruit salad." The name may have come from Carmen Miranda's famous number, "The Lady in the Tutti-Frutti Hat" in the 1943 movie *The Gang's All Here*, but Judy Rudoe in *Cartier 1900–1939* states that "... this has nothing to do with Cartier's gemstone jewelry."[3] Wherever the name came from, it was so pervasive that, in 1989, Cartier registered "Tutti Frutti" as a trademark.[4]

The engraved gemstones the house of Cartier used were imported from India. By the early 1910s, they had established a network of buying agents in Delhi, Calcutta, and Bombay that enabled them to procure rare Indian stones, including precious gemstones naturalistically engraved in leaf, blossom, and berry shapes. The decoration of these stones was based on the Islamic flower cult of the Mughal emperors and inspired Cartier's designers, Charles Jacqueau in Paris and Georges

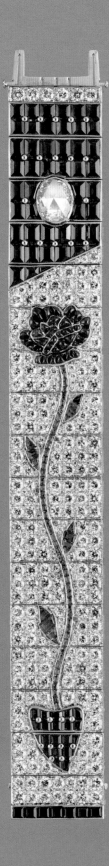

Genaille in New York, to create jewelry with engraved flowers and fruits. These gemstones were not as valuable as perfectly cut stones but the polychromatic effects on the jewelry were so striking that they became sought after by discriminating clients such as Mrs. Cole Porter, wife of the famous American composer, Mrs. W. K. Vanderbilt, and Mrs. William Randolph Hearst (p. 84).

The decoration on Tutti Frutti bracelets was normally designed as a stylized vine in which flowers and leaves grew from a branch embellished with diamonds. Usually rubies, emeralds, and sapphires were juxtaposed to give an interesting color palette but each jewel was different both in choice of gemstones and in their specific arrangement. On a bracelet, the stones appear as if placed at random but, on closer look, one sees that they were carefully positioned to give a massing effect of various shapes, textures, and colors (p. 84, top). Another bracelet composed of similar elements has a large engraved emerald set as a focal point to counterbalance the other slightly smaller emeralds at either end (p. 84, bottom). A Cartier bracelet with an engraved sapphire at the center adapts the Tutti Frutti theme. Instead of a polychromatic blending of gemstones, blues and greens dominate, a combination inspired by the colors of the Ballets Russes (p. 84, center). The unusual design of this bracelet features a band tapering from the engraved central sapphire to the clasp; the use of an engraved sapphire with a floral motif is rare.

For the 1925 Exposition Internationale des Arts Décoratifs et Industriels Modernes, both Lacloche Frères and Van Cleef & Arpels exhibited jewelry with floral motifs. Lacloche showed a selection of brooches and bracelets with flowers carved out of jade, coral, and moonstones.[5] Van Cleef & Arpels exhibited three examples of floral jewelry. One bracelet was designed with a garland of flowers and the other featured red and white roses (p. 81). The latter bracelet, a very ingenious design, was fashioned with six alternating roses, each with a diamond in the center; three with white diamonds and three with rubies, the petals of each overlapping the border. To add interest, the red roses are partially cut out from the background, making the flowers seem to float above the frame. The designer of this bracelet took a flat band and, with caprice, made it three-dimensional, somewhat challenging the rectilinear precepts of the period.

The third piece in their display at the exposition was a brooch that was designed in an artful manner with two fully open flowerheads, one in faceted diamonds and the other in buff-top rubies, each set with a diamond, yellow on the red rose and white on the white rose (p. 86). It, like the above-mentioned bracelet, is a tour de force of design that does not conform faithfully to the Art Deco canon. Nevertheless, for their spectacular rose jewelry, Van Cleef & Arpels was awarded a Grand Prix at the exposition.[6]

As the Art Deco period began to wane, the hard edges of the style began to soften. Floral jewelry once again took on a more three-dimensional appearance, returning to naturalistic blossoms such as a fuchsia brooch with buff-top rubies and yellow and white diamonds by Van Cleef & Arpels (p. 87). This brooch, with its hanging pistils and upturned petals, was a manifestation of the beginning of the new, bolder style of the next decade.

Opposite: A pictorial bracelet by Tiffany & Co. c. 1925, depicts a buff-cut ruby rose on a long emerald stem set into a square-cut-ruby vase over an articulated pavé diamond background. One end of the bracelet features a large crown rose-cut diamond on a background of calibré-cut sapphires.

Four important French articulated straight-line diamond Art Deco bracelets feature floral motifs. From top to bottom: Buff-cut sapphire chrysanthemums with emerald leaves and onyx branches display a Japanese influence, from Janesich. Abstract flowers form a wave background representing a stylized garden, from Rubel Frères in diamonds, calibré-cut onyx, sapphires, emeralds, and rubies. Flower and leaf motifs in buff-cut rubies, sapphires, purple sapphires, and emeralds alternate with onyx and emerald bands on a bracelet from Mauboussin. Semi-circular motifs with stylized rosettes are highlighted with calibré-cut rubies, sapphires, emeralds, and onyx against a diamond background on a bracelet by Van Cleef & Arpels.

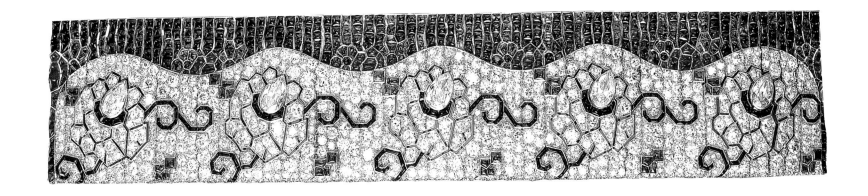

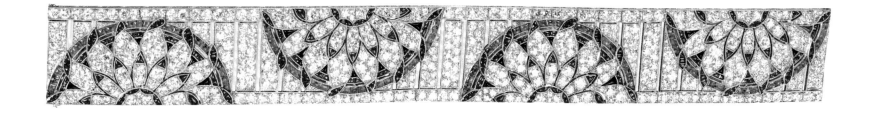

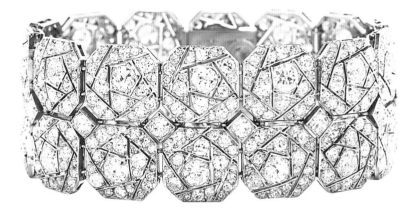

Opposite: This necklace by Boucheron is constructed of a long articulated band featuring blossoming calibré-cut ruby roses, accented with onyx, on a trellis. The band crosses over and fastens to form the asymmetrical necklace. This necklace was exhibited in the firm's display at the 1925 Exposition Internationale des Arts Décoratifs et Industriels Modernes in Paris.

Left: This articulated bracelet constructed of diamond roses was made by Marzo, Paris, c. 1925. Below: A straight-line bracelet by Lacloche Frères, c. 1925, features a line of roses and leaves in buff-cut rubies and emeralds. Bottom: A bracelet of six roses, three of diamonds and three of buff-cut rubies, with calibré-cut emerald leaves was exhibited in Van Cleef & Arpels's display at the 1925 Exposition Internationale des Arts Décoratifs et Industriels Modernes.

Left: A jabot brooch in the Tutti Frutti style features two large engraved emerald leaves and is accented by diamonds, rubies, and sapphire beads set in platinum. It was made for Mrs. Vincent Astor in 1927. Right: Cartier created this diamond and turquoise *sûreté* pin, c. 1925.

Three French Art Deco hardstone, platinum, and diamond bracelets feature floral motifs in the Japanese style, c. 1925. This rock crystal bracelet with diamonds, rubies and emeralds is attributed to Boucheron (top). A bracelet by Ernst Paltscho from Vienna is designed with flowers overlaid on a lapis background (middle). This Boucheron bracelet features jasper, turquoise, and enamel (bottom).

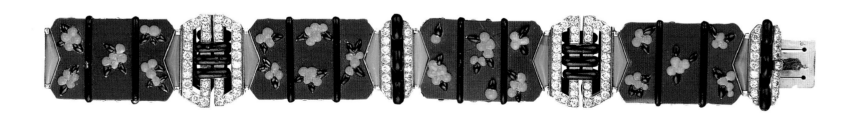

Four important Tutti Frutti bracelets by Cartier, Paris dating to the end of the 1920s are made with an assortment of engraved rubies, emeralds, and sapphires, and are highlighted with diamonds. This watch bracelet features an emerald crystal (opposite). This strap bracelet was formerly in the collection of Mrs. Cole Porter (top). This tapered bracelet in only two color tones using sapphires and emeralds features a large hexagonal sapphire engraved with a floral design based on the Islamic flower cult of the Moghul emperors. It was formerly in the collection of Millicent Hearst (middle). This bracelet features a large engraved emerald and pavé diamond branches (bottom).

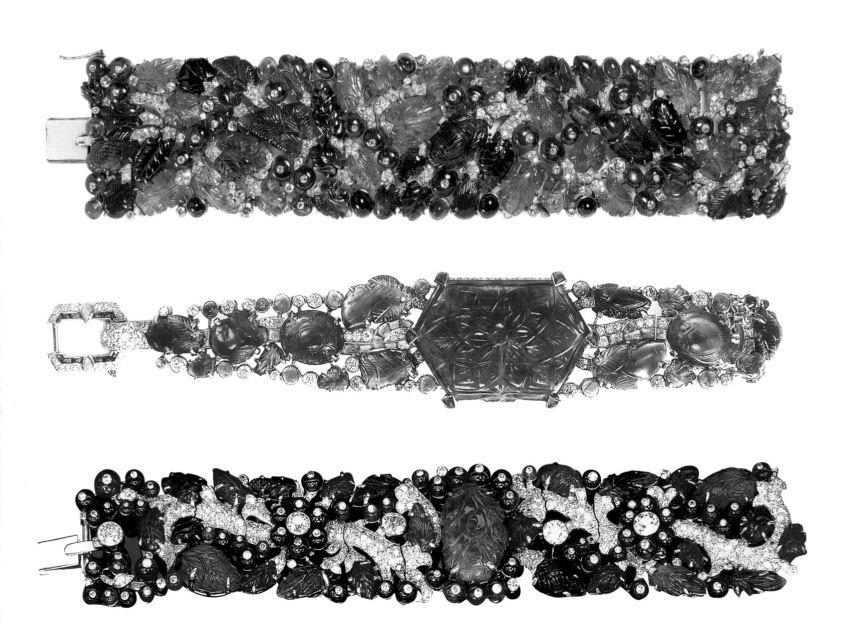

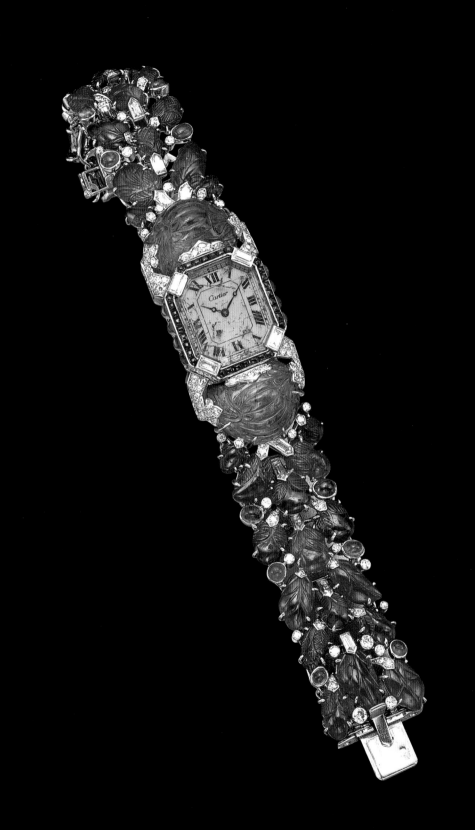

Left: Archival drawings depict two rose brooches from the Van Cleef & Arpels archives. The drawing at the bottom is the original design for the double rose clip brooch (right) in buff-cut rubies, diamonds, yellow diamond, emeralds, and onyx that the firm exhibited at the 1925 Exposition Internationale des Arts Décoratifs et Industriels Modernes.

Opposite: This platinum and gold, buff-cut ruby, yellow and white diamond fuchsia brooch by Van Cleef & Arpels from 1927 was illustrated on the cover of one of the firm's catalogues.

VAN CLEEF
& ARPELS
JOAILLIERS
22, Place Vendôme
PARIS

This Cartier, Paris, palm tree from 1939 was inspired by explorations in Africa and Asia during the 1920s and 1930s. While the leaves are set with circular and baguette diamonds to emphasize the various textures present in nature, the coconuts suspended from the branches are large briolette diamonds.

CHAPTER FOUR

The Thirties and Forties
Naturalism and Art Moderne Confections

The decades of the 1930s and 1940s proved to be a very exciting time in jewelry design in spite of the adverse environment created by the worldwide depression and the Second World War, both of which, ultimately, became major factors determining which jewelers continued making jewelry into the second half of the century and which did not. Responding to this time of adversity, successful jewelers pursued two seemingly divergent, yet complementary, paths: one returning to realism that had carried the day in the nineteenth century and the other reinterpreting jewelry in less traditional ways, using innovative techniques and materials. A new, vibrant style emerged with splashes of color and new materials, created by young designers forging new paths. It was a time of experimentation, of creating new identities very different from the past decade but not forgetting the successes of previous ones. This was especially evident in botanical jewelry, designed either in a naturalistic manner or in the art moderne style with abstractions of actual plants rendered not two-dimensionally, as in the 1920s, but three-dimensionally. Flowers were fun, often amusing, and proved to be a welcome respite during those difficult times.

The shift took place gradually. At the beginning of the 1930s, jewelry continued to reflect the rectilinear lines of Art Deco such as on a topiary brooch by Van Cleef & Arpels in which all the parts are put together with diamonds in geometric forms: navette-shape branches, trapezoidal trunk, and pentagonal tree top (p. 92). A brooch with two palm trees growing on a desert island incorporates baguette diamonds for the trunks and round and calibré-cut diamonds on the pinnate leaves (p. 90). This example shows a definite trend toward freer form and overall realism.

This palm tree brooch is set with round and baguette diamonds with calibré-cut emeralds accenting the leaves, c. 1930.

The Tutti Frutti style, which was so popular in the previous decade, continued into the 1930s but, again, within an expanded design freedom. Daisy Fellowes, known for her extraordinary sense of style, took three pieces of jewelry to Cartier to have made into a "Hindu" necklace, which was later readapted into its present form (p. 96). Van Cleef & Arpels updated the style further by arranging the gemstones in a more conventional configuration with a zig-zag pattern of engraved emerald flowers, alternately set with sapphire buds and ruby leaves (p. 98).

The new freedom encouraged imaginative variations on the Tutti Frutti style. As an alternative to demarcating each flower and leaf, some designers opted to unite several engraved elements to form what would appear to be one unit, as on a French necklace and ear clips whose engraved ruby leaves are joined together and topped with three small ruby beads to soften the carved elements (p. 97). Each of the decorative sections is set atop a diamond-set pentagonal formation, providing a splash of red to counterbalance the iciness of the diamonds.

By the early part of the 1930s, Cartier boldly adapted their style to the new design idiom. Two prime examples are a bracelet from 1931 and a head ornament from 1934. The ingeniously designed bracelet strikes a successful balance between imitation of nature and novelty of form (p. 95). The band, formed by partially overlapping diamond-set petals, grows wider from the ends to the center where the petals form two concentric circles that surround a flowerhead set with a diamond. The overall ensemble gives the impression of a flower whose petals emanate outward. The flowerhead centerpiece can be detached and worn independently as a brooch.

Cartier revamped the concept of a head ornament, making it suitable for the softer, wavier hair styles of the 1930s. Worn vertically on top of the head, it gave the impression of a halo when viewed from the front. One such head ornament was designed in the Egyptian style with lotus blossoms decreasing in size from the center to the tips (p. 93). What makes this piece so special is the dynamic design. At first glance, it appears to be a traditional head ornament but closer examination reveals subtle unusual details. Each blossom is supported by a straight stem set with two baguette diamonds and is flanked by free-standing elements canted inward from either side, adding a sense of movement within the composition. This effect is reinforced by the outward bending elements flanking the large blossom at the top of the piece.

Perhaps the one style most associated with floral jewelry from the 1930s are those pieces made in *serti invisible*, the invisible-setting technique, introduced by Van Cleef & Arpels in 1935. As simple as this technique appears to the casual observer, its execution is quite demanding and the result can be a masterpiece of the jeweler's art. To implement it, matched gemstones are cut into special shapes with four additional facets to provide a contrast of light and shade. The cut stones are then slid into grooves in a special mounting grid whereby each fits so snugly next to the other that no metal is visible. In *serti invisible* designs, stones can be cut into a variety of shapes such as trapeziums, triangles, or polygons that, when slotted into the mounting, create elegant sculptural works of art with flexible, planar, or three-dimensional surfaces. Petals on flower brooches undulate in a rippling motion while leaves curl and twist similarly to actual plants. Van Cleef & Arpels created roses and peonies as well as holly leaves in this technique (pp. 100–1). Immediately successful when first offered, they were acquired by such style setters of the decade as the Duchess of Windsor and King Farouk of Egypt.

By the end of the 1930s, naturalistically designed flowers, true to size and to realistic detail, had regained their previous popularity, often helped by a renewed emphasis on color. Flowers were made to look as natural specimens "dipped" in diamonds and other precious gemstones, much as they had been in the nineteenth century. Mauboussin's 1938 necklace of two rose blossoms came complete with leaves forming the center part of the bouquet (p. 104). Marcus & Co. slightly modified the double-rose theme by setting one blossom with rubies and the other with diamonds with green enameled leaves and stems for realism as well as contrast (p. 105, center). Paul Flato, an American maker whose jewelry was worn by stage and screen stars, crafted an all-white diamond brooch with one rose in full bloom and one just beginning to bud (p. 105, right). When pinned to the shoulder, both of these examples resemble an actual floral corsage. However, the really innovative corsage jewel of this time period was not one that replicated the actual flower but rather a special device Flato offered in 1934. It was decorated with diamond-set motifs and, when clipped shut, held a bouquet of real flowers (p. 108, right). It was described at the time as, "A jewel of distinctive charm and practicality, combining the luxurious softness of living flowers with the ever enduring beauty of precious stones."[1]

Oscar Heyman & Brothers, manufacturing jewelers in New York City, created jewelry for many firms including Bailey, Banks & Biddle; Marcus & Co.; Shreve & Co.; Shreve, Crump & Low; Tiffany & Co., and Udall & Ballou. In 1936, they made the first of their diamond-set gardenias, which they sold to Marcus & Co. and to Brand-Chatillon, a New York retailer located on the corner of Fifth Avenue and Fifty-fifth Street (p. 102).[2] This flower, along with their signature pansy[3] which dates to the same year, have remained popular ever since they were first introduced. They epitomize the credo of the firm's founder, Oscar Heyman, that "Jewelry should never be a candidate for redesign but should transcend time like a fine painting, never losing its appeal."[4]

The palm tree which had been rendered in a flatter, more two-dimensional style at the beginning of the decade, now is treated with full attention to detail, from the fibrous remains of the leaves covering the trunk to the plethora of leaves above. Cartier depicted this visual "feast for the eyes" in an all-diamond-set palm tree with circular and baguette-cut diamonds for the trunk and leaves and briolette diamonds for the coconuts (p. 88).

Some of the most artful floral jewels were those of rosebuds. Oscar Heyman & Brothers made a more traditional brooch with two buds (p. 105, left) while Flato offered it in a more dramatic way on a bracelet (p. 103). The bracelet is designed as a segment of a climbing rose bush with rosebuds

Suzanne Belperron designed this platinum and diamond abstract brooch, reminiscent of banana leaves, in the late 1930s.

entwined around a serpentine branch. The buds are set with round and single-cut diamonds, accented with (but, of course!) rose-cut diamonds. It is a truly artful play of design and choice of gem cut.

The theme of climbing plants reached its summit in a necklace of ivy leaves and flowers that wind around the neck (p. 106). Each leaf is pavéd with diamonds with the veins demarcated by open slits while the flower shoots in the actual plant have been replaced with five-petaled flowers, each set with a diamond. This unsigned necklace was originally owned by the actress Norma Shearer. It was designed by George Headley for Laykin et Cie, Los Angeles, between 1942 and 1945.[5]

Towards the end of the 1930s, as an alternative to the realistic treatment of flora, some jewelers were inspired by the moderne art trend in which flowers were represented in stylizations of actual blooms. Arthur Barney, silver designer for Tiffany & Co., created two flower jewels for the firm's exhibit at the 1939 World's Fair in New York. One was a diamond-and-ruby orchid rendered in a two-dimensional manner in contrast to the full-fledged enameled beauties that Paulding Farnham had designed for the 1889 Exposition Universelle in Paris.[6] The other piece was a stylized gold flower, species unknown, imaginatively designed with its center formed of baguette emeralds, topped with yellow and white diamonds, out of which spring four gold petals, each set with white diamonds at the tips, and three leaves made up of circular-cut yellow diamonds and baguette emeralds (p. 111).

The New York jeweler Seaman Schepps interpreted the modernist style in a simpler, more colorful manner on a bracelet that is composed of five flowers made up of gold petals that surround only half of the cabochon sapphire at the center, giving the illusion of an entire blossom (p. 124). Cabochon gemstones were a hallmark of Schepps's style, one that he consistently employed on his jewelry designs, such as on a bunch of grapes where the fruit is represented by a set of color-compatible cabochon sapphires (p. 125).

Sapphires had become popular in the late 1930s, used by other jewelers but in a very different way. In 1938, Van Cleef & Arpels introduced the passe-partout clips that were composed of two or three flowers with petals of cushion-cut Ceylon sapphires in yellow, blue, and pink. They could be worn on a suit lapel or attached to a gold gas-pipe chain worn around the necklace or coiled around the wrist (p. 120–1). On the other side of the Atlantic, Oscar Heyman & Brothers made a striking selection of flower jewelry in 1943 with various colored sapphires as the dominant stones (p. 109, right).

Jewelry from the last few years of the 1930s and the beginning of the 1940s is characterized by color, achieved not with the use of enameling, as had been the case at the turn of the century, but with gemstones. Up until that time, the major suppliers of those gemstones had been Burma, Thailand, and Indochina. The advent of the Second World War seriously curtailed those trade routes

A diamond-set bellflower brooch
captures the actual blossoming of the
plant with ten flowers cascading
downward. It is by the Parisian jeweler
Marchak, c. 1935.

and Brazil emerged as the supplier of choice, becoming a ready source of colored gemstones, particularly amethysts and aquamarines. Cartier utilized these stones to their fullest potential, creating an orchid with faceted fancy-cut aquamarines and amethysts (p. 115).

The house of Boivin had included orchids as part of their floral repertoire since the turn of the century, the first designed by René Boivin in 1905. By 1936, the flower had evolved into a pavé-set white and yellow diamond cattleya orchid, faithfully capturing the three-dimensionality of the variety; two years later, they replicated it with diamonds and rubies for Daisy Fellowes[7] (p. 115). In 1945, Juliette Moutard, a designer for the firm, created a suite of lily jewelry for Princess Irène of Greece,[8] consisting of a flowerhead clip brooch and a pair of earrings with pavé-set diamonds on the furled petals and calibré-cut ruby spray pistils (p. 114).

Beginning her career as a jewelry designer for Boivin, Suzanne Belperron left in 1933 to establish her own salon, producing work under the name of Herz at 59 rue de Châteaudun. She was a trendsetter, breaking with tradition to formulate a style that became uniquely her own. Whereas other jewelers were still relying principally on gold and platinum set with precious gemstones, she followed a different path, creating jewelry in which nontraditional gem material played a dominant role. Blue chalcedony, smoky agate, rock crystal, and ivory formed the actual jewel while gold, platinum, and gemstones played essential but subsidiary roles, such as on a brooch in which blue chalcedony is fashioned into a flowerhead with gold balls set with rubies at the center (p. 123, bottom). Her camellia has petals of carved chalcedony with the center of the blossom decorated with diamonds set into platinum (p. 123, top). On another brooch, ivory forms two leaves with gold serving as the stem and veins while five coral berries contribute a focal point as well as a dramatic splash of color (p. 123, left).

Another new and inventive designer, Fulco di Verdura, who worked with Paul Flato from 1937 to 1939, opened his own salon at 712 Fifth Avenue in New York City. To Verdura, design was always paramount, taking precedence over the intrinsic value of the gemstones. He drew inspiration from nature, interpreting it in his own, unique way. Instead of presenting a leaf in the traditional manner set with diamonds, he envisioned it in the autumn, "painting" the reds, greens, browns, and yellows in zircons, tourmalines, Mali garnets, and fire opals (p. 116, left). To be more faithful to nature, Verdura deliberately chose an imperfectly formed leaf for this jewel; the top quarter of the leaf on the left side is not bifurcated as it is on the right side.[9]

The palm tree, which had been a favored image in 1930s, metamorphosed into an abstract three-dimensional version of the plant by the end of the 1940s. Cartier produced a necklace with ruby beads arranged into two bunches of coconuts, supported by branches connected to the tree trunk (p. 126). A variant on this theme is seen on a brooch by the same firm in which four pinnate leaves, each set with a diamond at the end, support the fruit above, made out of sapphire beads (p. 126).

A 1931 platinum and diamond bracelet with a detachable flower-clip brooch is shown with Cartier publicity of the period showing the bracelet.

Cartier *Ltd*

175, NEW BOND STREET, LONDON

This Tutti Frutti necklace was made by
Cartier, Paris for Daisy Fellowes in 1936.
Although the design was modified from
the previous decades, it still retains essential elements characteristic of the style.

A variation on the Tutti Frutti style is this French necklace and pair of ear clips with groups of engraved rubies and ruby beads on rectilinear segments, c. 1935.

Below top: These 1930s designs from
Boucheron in the Tutti Frutti style display
a more symmetrical approach to the
polychromatic presentation of engraved
gemstones. Below bottom: This Van Cleef
& Arpels bracelet from 1937 is an example
of the Tutti Frutti style from the period.

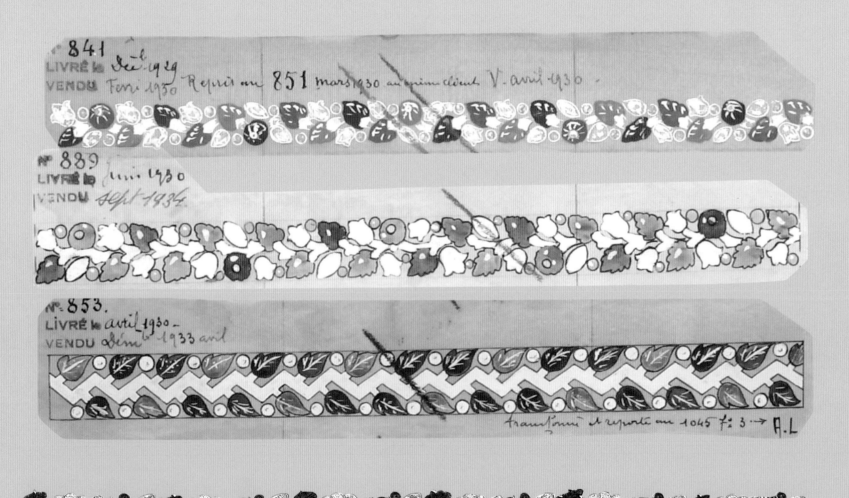

Jewelry with botanical motifs proliferated during the two decades of the 1930s and 1940s. Flat, rectilinear designs were quickly eclipsed by sculptural jewels in which the flower became integral to the design, either rendered in its naturalistic glory or depicted abstractly. Color came to the fore, not always in deep tones but often in paler shades. And new designers such as Boivin, Seaman Schepps, Paul Flato, Suzanne Belperron, and Fulco di Verdura introduced a new, vibrant design credo into jewelry fashion. It was a time of experimentation and of looking at flora through new eyes.

An engraved amethyst, sapphire bead and diamond brooch by Cartier, London, c. 1935, is an unusual adaptation of the Tutti Frutti style. Although the brooch is created in a foliate design, the shape actually resembles a *sarpech*, an Indian turban ornament.

Right: The earliest version of invisibly set jewels are seen in this advertisement sketch by René Sim Lacaze for Van Cleef & Arpels, 1937, and by the stylized ruby and diamond floral-spray brooch. In this technique, the rubies are ingeniously held in place by gold wires that fit into grooves on the sides of the calibré-cut stones. The leaves are made of baguette-cut diamonds. Below: This design by Boucheron from 1939 is for a brooch with similar invisibly set ruby and diamond flowers.

Top: Arguably the most spectacular example of invisibly set jewelry is this rose brooch from Van Cleef & Arpels with twenty-five petals made of rubies and two leaves of emeralds with diamond veins, all set in gold and platinum. Made in 1938, its royal provenance is that of the Court of Egypt under King Farouk. Right: A Van Cleef & Arpels 1937 archival drawing depicts an invisibly set ruby and diamond peony double clip brooch. Left: The most famous example of invisibly set jewels is the 1937 holly clip made by Van Cleef & Arpels for the Duchess of Windsor. It is made with pavé diamonds on one leaf and invisibly set rubies on the other.

Right: This gardenia brooch in diamonds, with green enamel leaves was made by the American manufacturing jeweler Oscar Heyman & Brothers in 1937 for the Los Angeles retailer Brock & Co. Left: These platinum-and-diamond earrings in the form of a five-petal flower are French and date to the mid 1930s. Bottom: This bracelet by Van Cleef & Arpels from 1937 features diamond blossoms with yellow diamond pistils, stems in baguette diamonds, berries in rubies, and baguette-emerald leaves.

Right: Rose-cut diamonds form the center of rosebuds entwined on a serpentine branch set with baguettes on this meandering articulated bracelet by Paul Flato from the late 1930s. Below top: White and yellow diamond flowers with ruby accents are scattered on a diamond-set scroll by the New York jeweler Raymond Yard, c. 1935. Below bottom: Max Halpern, head of one of the best jewelry workshops in Paris, created this brooch in the 1940s with two diamond flowers, each with yellow diamond pistils, and emerald leaves and ribbon.

Above: An elaborate platinum double-rose necklace Mauboussin created for Queen Nazli of Egypt in 1938 is composed of three-dimensional blossoms realized in pavé-set diamonds with baguette accents.

Top: Although not known for his realistic portrayal of flowers, Paul Flato created this single blossom and bud diamond-set rose brooch at the end of the 1930s. Below: A rose brooch with one blossom in calibré-cut rubies and another in diamonds, and a bud also in diamonds, was designed by Marcus & Co. The leaves and stems are in green enamel, an innovative twist introduced by American jewelers in the 1930s. Left: In 1937 Oscar Heyman & Brothers created a brooch of two diamond-set rosebuds with enameled leaves.

This polished-gold and diamond necklace featuring cascading ivy leaves on a semi-rigid form that dates to the late 1940s belonged to the actress Norma Schearer. It was designed by George Headley for Laykin et Cie, Los Angeles, between 1942 and 1945.

Mimosa clips in polished gold and set
with diamonds were made by Van Cleef &
Arpels in 1948. Princess Soraya, the wife
of the Shah of Iran in the early 1950s,
is wearing the clips in the accompanying
portrait.

Below: A brooch by F. Walter Lawrence, Inc. of New York from c. 1945 features a bouquet of enameled daisies, each with a diamond in the center. A diamond-set butterfly with demantoid garnets on its wings, a pearl for its upper body, and ruby eyes, has just alighted onto it. Right: A Paul Flato advertisement from *Harper's Bazaar*, May 1934, features a unique diamond-set device that, when clipped shut, holds a bouquet of live blossoms.

HAT AND GOWN BY BERGDORF GOOD

PATENT PENDING

THE CORSAGE PIN A
GREATLY DESIRED
AND NOW ESSENTIAL PART OF EVERY
WOMAN'S CHIC —— DESIGNED BY
PAUL FLATO AS A JEWEL OF DISTINC-
TIVE CHARM AND PRACTICABILITY,
COMBINING THE LUXURIOUS SOFTNESS
OF LIVING FLOWERS WITH THE EVER
ENDURING BEAUTY OF PRECIOUS STONES.

PAUL E. FLATO, INC.
JEWELLERS
ONE EAST 57TH STREET
NEW YORK

Top: Another twist on the floral bouquet by Oscar Heyman & Brothers from 1943 is a brooch with multicolored sapphires accented with rubies and sapphires on polished gold leaves and with a diamond-set ribbon. The flowers here border on the abstract, since the petals are made from square cut stones. Right: On a brooch in the form of a bouquet by Oscar Heyman & Brothers from the mid 1940s, the flowers are made from various shades of blue and yellow sapphires, accented with diamonds. Left: Van Cleef & Arpels designed this bouquet brooch in 1947 using large light-blue sapphires for the floral petals and small rubies for the center. It is surrounded by ruffled lace in polished open-work gold.

Right: Jewelry sketches from Boucheron for abstract bouquet brooches in gold are by a young designer, Pierre Sterlé, who worked briefly at Boucheron during the 1940s. He later opened his own firm on Avenue de l'Opéra in Paris, producing highly inventive jewelry in the next two decades. Below: A pair of lotus-blossom ear clips by Cartier, Paris, dates to c. 1938. They are set with a single diamond at the center of each flower while diamonds encircle the stem, a feature that is not readily visible when worn. Below bottom: An American bracelet with ten undulating leaves that appear to fall over a "hidden" branch. The center of each leaf is set with either diamonds or rubies.

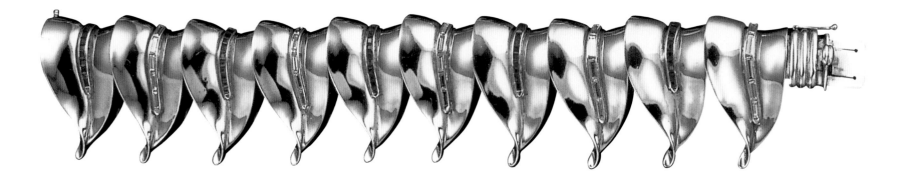

Top: Made for the 1939 World's Fair in New York by Tiffany & Co., this floral brooch in gold, diamonds, and emeralds presages the style trends of the 1940s with its use of polished gold leaves and ribbon-like stems. Below: A variation of the ever-popular rose brooch is this version by Trabert & Hoeffer, Inc.-Mauboussin from their "Reflection: Your Personality in a Jewel" line from the late 1930s. It is set with diamonds and rubies. Bottom left: A 1940s version on the ever-popular orchid with a ruby pistil, pavé-diamond petals, and polished-gold leaves.

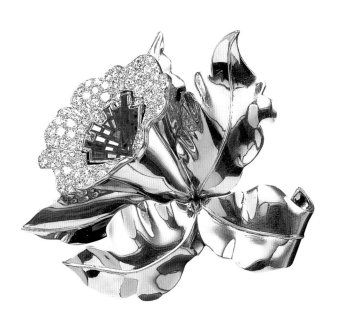

Left: Two sketches for raspberry brooches are by Boucheron, c. 1942. Left bottom: These two rings, made by Anna Bachelli from Turin, in bombé form depict a ripened and unripened blackberry, one in cabochon rubies and the other in cabochon black onyx. Toledo Museum of Art. Below: A three-piece suite by Boucheron, c. 1948, consists of a brooch and pair of earrings in platinum and diamonds with the insides of the flower heads in guilloché with transparent enamel.

Opposite: A page from the Boucheron archives, 1941, shows sketches for floral jewels. Note the boxes that record the dates each model was entered into stock and sold.

Opposite: A suite consisting of a large clip brooch and pair of earrings in the form of lilies by René Boivin was made in 1945. The petals are old mine-cut diamonds set in gold and the pistils are calibré-cut rubies.

Below left: Faceted fancy-cut amethysts and aquamarines make an unusual combination for this large, stylized orchid brooch by Cartier, Paris, a special order in 1937. The white gold settings are camouflaged by pale-blue and mauve enamel studs between the stones. Below right: This three-dimensional large orchid brooch was made by René Boivin in 1938 in pavé diamonds and calibré-cut and round rubies set in polished gold.

Right: A suite in the form of leaves by René Boivin was made in 1938. Tourmalines ranging from greens and golds to pinks suggest the changing colors of autumn leaves. Each round stone is cleverly mounted within oval settings to give character to the composition. Below right: Suzanne Belperron made this abstract floral brooch with multicolored sapphires surrounding a large aquamarine, c. 1945. For contrast on this piece, Belperron included an engraved emerald leaf near two polished gold leaves on the stem. Below left: The maple-leaf brooch by Fulco di Verdura was first created in the 1940s. Various colored zircons, tourmalines, mali garnets, and fire opals combine to produce a realistic interpretation of typical autumn colors.

Opposite right: A citrine and pavé diamond lotus flower brooch mounted in 18K gold and platinum was made by Cartier, London, c. 1935. Opposite middle: This pair of emerald and diamond thistle brooches were created by René Boivin in 1934. They were formerly in the collection of H.R.H. Irène, Queen of Greece and Denmark. Opposite bottom: A gold and diamond flower double-clip brooch by René Boivin from 1940 is in the form of tulip heads. They are worn upside down on the shoulder like an actual corsage. Opposite left: A pink tourmaline and green garnet foxglove brooch was designed by Juliette Moutard in 1944 for René Boivin. Like many Boivin jewels, the flower heads move when worn.

Two matching gold cuff bracelets with detachable sapphire clips in a floral motif surrounded by diamond leaves set in platinum were made by the Parisian jeweler Ostertag, around 1940.

Left: This large-scale diamond-set flower clip brooch by Cartier was a special order in 1941. The flexible stem moves when worn. Middle: This large and important flower brooch was made by Cartier, New York in 1941. The stem is set with square-cut emeralds and the flower petals are made in faceted sapphires, accented with diamond scrolls set in platinum. Below: This pair of bouquet brooches in emeralds, sapphires, and diamonds was made on special order by Cartier, London in 1946. Note the two briolette emeralds on each brooch that depict leaves.

Chapeau en or tressé, orné d'un bouquet de saphirs, rubis et brillants, porté avec un bracelet et un collier assortis. Ensemble spécialement créé pour l'Exposition de New-York par

A 1939 advertisement from Van Cleef & Arpels for the passe-partout jewels shows how chic this line of jewelry looked when worn. Large yellow or light-blue sapphires form the petals of the flowers, centering on a nucleus of rubies or dark-blue sapphires. The flowers are detachable clips that could be worn separately or attached to gold gas-pipe chains of varying lengths. In the advertisement, the long gas pipe is worn as a necklace or wrapped several times to form a bracelet. A necklace version shows five clips on a shorter gas-pipe chain (opposite).

V A N   C L E E F   &   A R P E L S
2 2 ,   P L A C E   V E N D O M E ,   P A R I S

Top: A rose brooch by Cartier, Paris from 1941 is made of carved coral in the form of a flower with the edges of the petals enhanced with diamonds. Below right: A rose brooch in carved angel-skin coral is enhanced with gold leaves. Below left: A carved coral rose blossom is mounted into diamond-set leaves by Van Cleef & Arpels from the late 1940s.

During the 1940s, Suzanne Belperron created many floral brooches, sculpted from hardstones. The following is a selection: The camellia brooch (top) is made from carved chalcedony and decorated with a pavé diamond center. The leaves are represented by cabochon emeralds and mounted in 18K white gold. The eglantine flower brooch (right) features two agate leaves and five articulated petals of white agate. The pistil is set with diamonds and sugarloaf-cut coral, mounted in white gold. An ivory leaf brooch (left) was made with a gold stem and coral berries. The daisy on this brooch (bottom) was carved from a single blue chalcedony and set with rubies mounted in gold at the center.

Right: This Cartier brooch from the 1940s is in the form of a tree growing from a faceted aquamarine pot. The centers of the flowers are blue, yellow, and purple sapphires with cabochon sapphire and ruby petals. Below: Seaman Schepps created this floral link bracelet in the early 1940s for client Emily Hall Tremaine. Stylized petals with fluted polished gold cups each hold a cabochon sapphire surrounded by diamond pistils. Cabochon rubies and emeralds complete the floral theme. It is shown with its original sketch.

Left: Moonstones form the catkins on this impressive pussy-willow brooch made by Tiffany & Co. in the early 1940s. Diamonds line the stems, providing a delicateness to the design. Below: A grape-bunch brooch made of different shades of cabochon sapphires by Seaman Schepps in 1941. Carved emerald leaves blend with a large pavé diamond leaf to give character to this popular theme. This brooch belonged to the American heiress Doris Duke. It is an adaptation of the archival drawing (left).

Right: A special order from Cartier, Paris in 1949, this necklace depicts a palm tree with cascading coconuts made of ruby beads studded with collet-set diamonds. The latticework brings to mind tropical weaving. Below: A similarly styled brooch by Cartier with palm fronds sports sapphire bead coconuts, topped with a diamond-set floral motif.

This Van Cleef & Arpels necklace was commissioned in 1949 by Her Highness the Maharani Sita Devi of Baroda. Known as "the Indian Wallis Simpson" for her second marriage to the Maharaja of Baroda and for her passion for jewelry, among the jewels she received from the Baroda treasury, dating back to Mughal times, were emerald drops that became part of this necklace. The central design of this necklace is a lotus flower; when it was completed in 1950, Van Cleef & Arpels christened it the "Hindu necklace."

The "Hedges and Rows" necklace, designed by Jean Schlumberger, was first introduced by Tiffany & Co. in 1960. It is set with cabochon turquoise, yellow sapphires, and diamonds set into platinum.

CHAPTER FIVE

The Fifties and Sixties

Glamorous Jet-Set Style

The two decades after the Second World War were a time of contrasts, of economic boom followed by controversy and dispute. After the war ended, much effort went into rebuilding what had been destroyed, fostering a time of affluence both in Europe and the United States. Overall, the mood was one of going back to tastes and values cherished before the big conflict forced major readjustments. Yet within that conservative mood, new times dictated new styles, especially in fashion with the "New Look" introduced by Christian Dior in 1947—a silhouette with rounded small shoulders, a heart-shaped neckline, and a narrow waist flaring out into an ample skirt.

The 1950s were a time of wonderment, of liberation from the anxieties of the past decade, a time when women loved to dress up in richly embroidered silks and laces for evening parties. Events such as the story-book pomp and circumstance of the highly publicized marriage of the American actress Grace Kelly to Prince Rainier III of Monaco on April 19, 1956, captivated the world. Then, by the end of the decade, the mood changed markedly and the 1960s became a time for casting off the old in search of the new. Andy Warhol and Roy Lichtenstein introduced imagery adapted from popular culture into the fine arts while, in fashion, elegance gave way to a simpler, more straightforward look. The style most associated with this decade was the mini skirt, popularized by Mary Quant. In the United States, the assassinations of President John F. Kennedy, his brother Robert, and Martin Luther King Jr., shocked the nation while the controversy over the Vietnam War divided the country. It was a time of turmoil but design did not fall victim to these circumstances. Perhaps as the citizenry felt free to speak out against what they thought was

Top right: The petals on the flowers of this pair of 1950s French gold and diamond earrings are made of woven gold that opens and closes to reveal or hide the diamond stamens. The diamond centers unscrew and are interchangeable with ruby or sapphire-set centers. Bottom right: These French gold and diamond flower earrings suspending tassels of gold chain date to the 1950s. Bottom left: A pair of flower head earrings in yellow and white diamonds were made by Van Cleef & Arpels, New York in the 1950s. Top left: These floral earclips in gold and diamonds by Pierre Sterlé were made in the early 1960s.

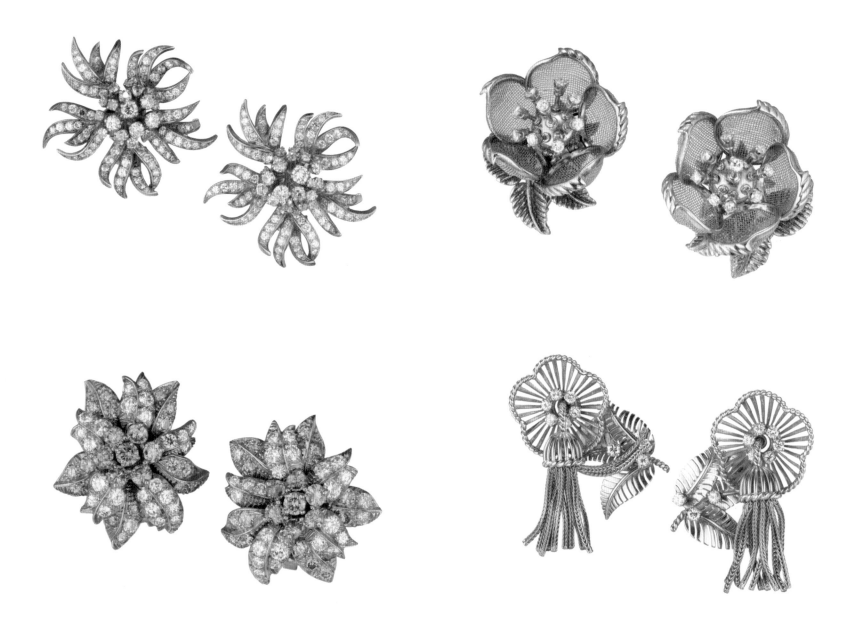

wrong, designers experienced renewed freedom to pursue new avenues of creativity, very prominently so in jewelry design.

Operating within this dynamic social environment, the jewelry styles of these two decades exhibited very different characteristics, with the conservatism of the 1950s giving way to the quirkiness of the 1960s. Floral and leaf motifs, for the most part similar to those of the 1940s, continued into the 1950s, while the turbulence and disaffection of the 1960s suggested a new design aesthetic with fruit and vegetable motifs—imagery not seen in jewelry since the end of the nineteenth century—playing important roles. In retrospect, both latter eras have much in common: an extended period of affluence as well as a burst of intellectual discovery and the introduction of new technology—the electric light bulb and the automobile at the turn of the century and space exploration in the 1960s, to name a few.

One aspect of 1950s jewelry that was a throwback to the nineteenth century was the resurrection of matching sets, called "parures" in the 1800s, consisting of brooch, earrings, and bracelet in diamonds and precious gemstones. Necklaces that had been formerly composed of intertwining leaves and flowers now took the shape of a bib in which the necklet, either woven in gold or made out of platinum and set with diamonds, supported the decorative detail at the front. All of the major Parisian houses created these ensembles. René-Sim Lacaze, the former artistic director working with Renée Puissant at Van Cleef & Arpels, made a floral suite for Mauboussin in 1950 in which the bib front features clusters of five-petaled flowers separated by gold batons breaking the regularity of the design (p. 132). In New York, Van Cleef & Arpels adapted the ivy-leaf theme with stylized heart-shape leaves twisting and turning to provide movement within the design. Three "stray" leaves cascade down from the center of the necklace while diamond-set flowers replicate the projecting

These leaf earrings by the Parisian jeweler Marchak date to the early 1950s and are constructed with gold wire studded with diamonds; pear-shape rubies dangle from the edges.

Page 132: Sketches by René-Sim Lacaze from the Mauboussin archives for a floral necklace and bracelet, part of a suite, in gold with diamonds and multicolored gemstones date to the early 1950s.

Page 133: This floral suite consisting of a necklace, bracelet, ring, and earrings was designed by René-Sim Lacaze for Mauboussin, Paris, c. 1960. Cabochon rubies form the centers of pavé diamond flowers surrounded by leaves of engraved emeralds.

Bottom right: A pair of gold earrings by Cartier were made in the form of coffee beans; the French term is *grains de café*. Versions of these were first made around 1953 for both the Paris and New York salons. Bottom left: Another pair of earrings by Cartier utilizes the *grains de Café* motif but the coffee beans are carved in coral and accented with diamonds.

flower shoots on the plant (p. 144). The Parisian jeweler Pierre Sterlé created a suite with five-petaled flowers of emeralds, sapphires, rubies, and diamonds set against a backdrop of three leaves (p. 137). Three groups make up the bib part of the necklace, with a large diamond-set flower in front of the leaves and smaller flowers in precious gemstones in between. As is characteristic of necklaces from the 1950s, single diamond-set loops provide the transition between the luscious central floral section and the single strand necklet, also diamond-set.

The traditional mood of the 1950s was in a look back to the styles of the 1930s by both jewelers and their clients, many of whom were less sensitive to the changes of fashion. Established classics such as Van Cleef & Arpels's invisibly set flowerhead brooches became popular again, accessorizing the "New Look" dresses (p. 143). The firm also created flowerhead brooches and ear clips in the guise of marguerites, also known as ox-eye daisies, with yellow and white diamonds making up the color palette on the capitula (opposite, top).

After a ten-year hiatus, the palm tree was revived but, instead of interpreting it in an abstract manner like examples from the late 1940s, Cartier and Bulgari designed models that more closely resembled the actual plant (p. 149). On both examples, the diamond cuts delineate the pinnate leaves with baguettes forming the rachis and rounds for the feathery fronds. On the Cartier palm tree, baguette-cut diamonds are set on a 90-degree angle on one side of three leaves, giving the effect of wind gently wafting through them.[1] The whiteness of the diamonds is offset with rubies on the Cartier piece and with sapphires on Bulgari's, which is also set with five marquise-cut diamonds for contrast.

Left: A pair of clip brooches representing ox-eye daisies by Van Cleef and Arpels was made in 1952. Made with yellow and colorless diamonds, the center colors contrast with that of the petals with each set portraying either a white or yellow daisy. Left: A diamond-set brooch with a sapphire at the center was made in the 1950s by McTeigue & Company, New York. Below: A suite of dahlias in emeralds and diamonds set in platinum was made by Villa, Milano around 1960.

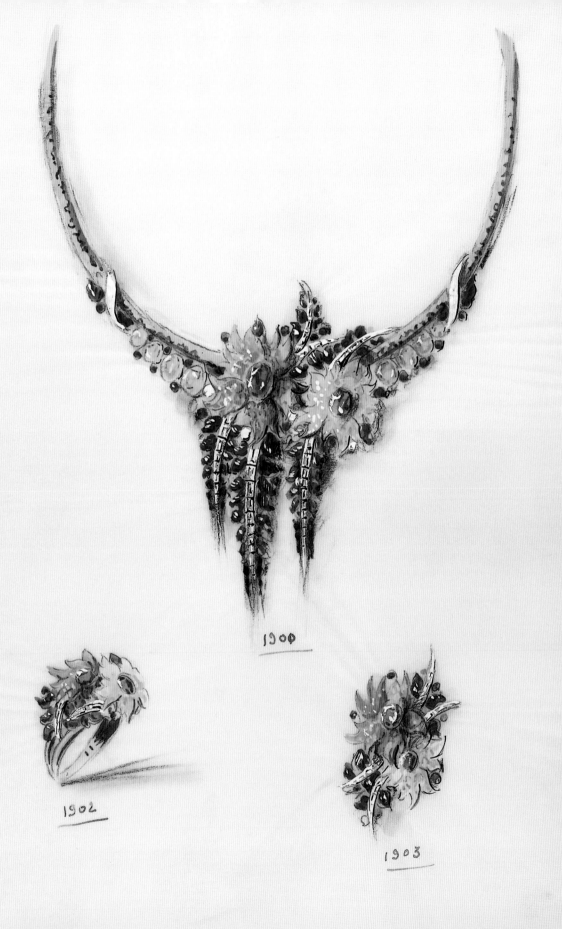

A design drawing by René-Sim Lacaze for Mauboussin, Paris, c. 1960, depicts a three-piece floral suite of necklace, brooch, and ring.

Opposite: This floral suite comprising a necklace, bracelet, earrings, and brooch in diamonds, emeralds, rubies, and sapphires was made by Pierre Sterlé in the late 1950s.

1900

1902

1903

Right: Pierre Sterlé created this suite depicting leaves consisting of earrings, a pair of brooches, and an unusual watch in 18K *cotte de mailles*, or knitted gold, c. 1951. Below top: This pair of emerald bead leaf earrings by Cartier was originally created in 1967 with diamonds along the edges and stem. In 1976, the diamonds were replaced with 100 emeralds. The earrings were purchased by Doris Duke at auction in 1991. Below bottom: These earrings by Jean Schlumberger for Tiffany & Co. have emerald and diamond leaves that rotate to reveal or hide the gemstones, 1959.

The bracelet of this suite, which also includes a brooch, ear clips, and ring, is inspired by an actual plant with flower and leaves making up the center part while the stems wind around the wrist. Made by Boucheron in the 1950s, each piece is set with diamonds in yellow gold for the flowers and leaves with black pearls at the centers of the flowers and white pearls for accent.

In 1955, Cartier, Paris, made this carved coral bellflower necklace set in platinum with beads of emeralds, onyx, and coral and with clasps of black enamel set with diamonds. Originally made as a bracelet, it was modified by Cartier as a necklace for the Mexican actress Maria Felix.

But the truly imaginative tree brooches from the 1950s that surpassed anything that had ever been done before were created on both sides of the Atlantic by two very different designers; Germaine Boivin in Paris and Julius Cohen in New York. Germaine Boivin was the youngest daughter of René Boivin and his wife, Jeanne, who continued the firm after her husband's death in 1917. She entered the firm as a designer in the 1920s, eventually taking over the company after her mother's death in 1959. Germaine, like her mother, created jewelry with unusual color combinations, more like an artist than a jeweler. For her mother's eightieth birthday, she designed a cedar-tree brooch fitted with a series of folding plaques engraved with the names of important designers, master jewelers, and associates who had worked closely with her parents over the years (p. 148, top). Its clever design features kite-cut amethysts for the roots, most likely symbolizing her parents as the founders of the company, pavé-set amethyst and pink tourmaline trunk that graduate in color to simulate shading on one side of the tree, demantoid garnets for the needle leaves arranged in tufts from which the amethyst and cabochon pink tourmaline cones grow. It is an ingenious reinterpretation of a family tree.

Julius Cohen, who opened a salon on East Fifty-third Street in New York City in 1955, enjoyed making inventive, whimsical jewelry, often with botanical themes. In his weeping willow brooch four textured gold stalks begin as roots, turn into the trunk and, at the top, split into branches pulled downward with the heavy burden of the peridot leaves (p. 148, bottom). In another inventive design for the Diamonds International Awards in 1957, Cohen created a nontraditional flower pot brooch in which gold stems in a series of "U" shapes are set with leaves of round and marquise diamonds with a pear shape crowning the top (p. 148, left). The most imaginative feature of this brooch is the flowerpot which is formed of a 4.15 carat portrait diamond, an unusual style in which the edges are bevel cut along the top and bottom, leaving a large table. He received an award for excellence of design for this piece.

Also famous for flower pot jewelry, Bulgari's design concept boasted precious gemstones set en masse, combining rubies and sapphires with diamonds or emeralds to simulate flowers in an arrangement, thus greatly enriching the visual impact of what could have been just pretty brooches. It was at that time that the firm began using cabochon-cut colored stones as a prominent element in their designs such as forming the pots in these brooches[2] (p. 151).

Another popular form of floral jewelry toward the end of the 1950s and 1960s were bouquets or posies, as they were sometimes called, especially those created with violets, flowers that had symbolized faithfulness in the nineteenth century. This associative quality was no longer the raison d'etre for their creation; rather, they were chosen for their simple beauty. Verdura designed such a bouquet with amethysts and diamonds and Boivin made two different versions, one with oval-cut amethysts and one with pink tourmalines (pp. 152-3). Tiffany & Co. created a somewhat more formal floral bouquet where the centers of the flowers are set with rubies and diamonds and a fancy

This brooch, made by Mauboussin, depicts a Parisian kiosk full of flowers of engraved rubies, sapphires, and emeralds, accented with diamonds, c. 1950.

yellow-brown diamond in the center of the arrangement adds an elegant touch, as does the diamond-set leaf holding the stems in place (p. 153).

By the beginning of the 1960s jewelry had become more inventive, more playful, with the use of unusual materials as well as new imagery, a reflection of the openness that was felt during this decade. Sterlé created a dahlia brooch but instead of a frontal view, he turned it halfway around, positioning it as if caught in the wind with billowing petals, some with their tips turned upward. The petals are not made with traditional gemstones but with mother-of-pearl[3] (p. 163).

During the late 1940s and 1950s, Jean Schlumberger formulated his well-known repertory of jewelry, drawing upon nature for inspiration. He joined Tiffany & Co. in 1956, breathing new life into the firm's designs. He drew upon nature for inspiration, especially images from the garden. In his words, "I try to make everything look as if it were growing, uneven, at random, organic, in motion. I want to capture the irregularity of the universe. I observe nature and find verve."[4] However, his depictions of flowers, leaves, fruits, and vegetables were often interpretations of general species rather than of actual plants. He looked at nature and interpreted it artistically, not literally. Superb examples of this approach are a necklace and matching earring suite that is designed with leaves but not precisely identifiable ones (p. 154) and the "Hedges and Rows" necklace, which is an adaptation of hedgerows that line the English countryside (p. 128).[5]

In the 1960s, the garden basket also included fruits and vegetables, often depicted as if freshly plucked from the plant. Schlumberger captured the strawberry in this manner with rubies set with gold prongs to replicate the achenes (p. 156). Donald Claflin, who started working at Tiffany's in 1965, designed jewelry with a sense of fun, a sense of flair. Instead of creating just one strawberry, he crafted a magnificent bracelet of the entire plant with diamond-set flowers with gold pistils, enameled green leaves and coral strawberries with gold achenes (p. 156). The Parisian firm of Marchak also looked at fruit in a novel way by designing a slice of watermelon with cabochon rubies that graduate in color, darker at the rind and lighter at the edge of the slice, and sapphires cut in the shape of seeds. The roughened texture of the rind simulates the underside of the fruit when it is on the ground, while the subtle detail of a vine that curls around the stem adds movement to what could have been a static design (p. 156). Fulco di Verdura first designed his ingenious pomegranates when he was working with Paul Flato but it was a motif he continued to rely on throughout his artistic life. On a brooch and matching earrings, he set the skin of the fruit with faceted peridots while letting cabochon rubies represent the edible pulp of the fleshy seeds (p. 157). David Webb, the New York designer who became known for his bold, striking jewelry, designed a bracelet with the grapevine motif, an image regularly resurrected in jewelry design every twenty years or so. Clusters of cabochon emerald grapes amid pavé-set diamond leaves with twisted gold vines create a refined version of the natural features of the actual plant (p. 161).

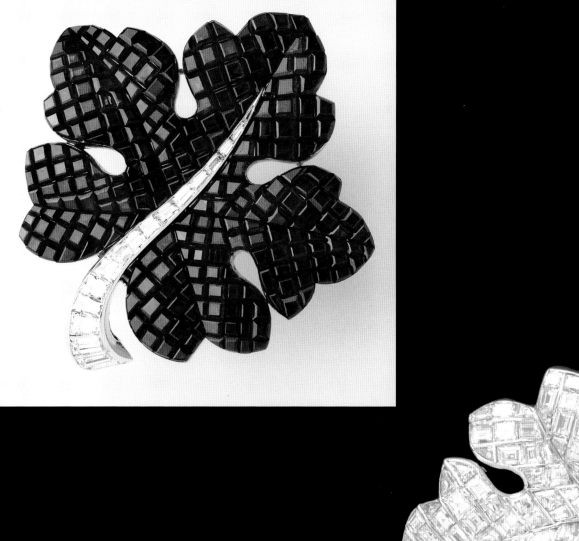
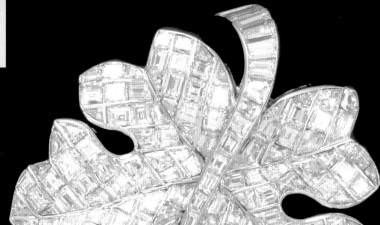

Opposite: This suite of light-colored sapphire leaves with diamond stems by Van Cleef & Arpels, New York dates to the beginning of the 1950s.

Left: Van Cleef & Arpels continued its tradition of making invisibly set jewels with this two-leaf clip from 1954 in diamonds and invisibly set sapphires. The two leaves separate to form two brooches. It is superimposed over a catalogue cover with an illustration of the jewel. Below: Diamond-set palm fronds on a pair of ear clips by Pierre Sterlé from the 1950s support drop pearls.

Although the vegetable cart hardly seems like an inspirational source for jewelry, two designers reached into it for ideas. When asked to create a special one-of-a-kind jewel for Armory Houghton using the client's own jade pea pods, Schlumberger acquiesced by designing a clip brooch with the pea pods hanging from leaves set with olivines (p. 159). Verdura was inspired by the mushroom, creating whimsical brooches from some phantasmal world with miniature pixies sitting underneath the caps, shielding themselves from the sun (p. 164). He was also fascinated by an ear of corn, still encased in its husk, with kernels made out of black pearls (p. 164).

Although deciduous trees and their leaves were frequently portrayed in jewelry design, evergreens and Christmas imagery were not seen until the 1950s and 1960s. Perhaps the texture of their leaves or needles or even the trees themselves were not conducive to traditional design. Verdura, who searched for the unusual, looked at this source with curiosity, creating a remarkably realistic pine-cone brooch in which the tips of the scales are pavé-set with diamonds (p. 165).

Christmas-themed designs first appeared in costume jewelry at the end of the Second World War[6] but it would take almost two decades before they would be realized in fine gemstones. In the 1960s, Jean-Claude Duhem, a Parisian manufacturing jeweler designed jewelry for Bulgari including a miniature Christmas tree with diamond-set garlands, cabochon emerald, ruby, and sapphire balls, and crowned by a diamond-set star (p. 165). In 1968, Oscar Heyman & Brothers fashioned a seasonal bracelet of holly leaves and berries (p. 165).

Within the two decades of the 1950s and 1960s, the traditional evolved into the innovative with imagery never before seen in jewelry. The ever beautiful flower proliferated along with trees, bouquets, fruits, vegetables, and seasonal designs. Overall, these were exciting times for renewal and innovation, times to take stock and times to forge ahead, leaving behind a rich legacy of splendid jewelry.

Opposite: This brooch in the form of a jonquil was designed by Frederick A. Mew of Cartier in 1952 for Queen Elizabeth II. Baguette-cut diamonds form the stem, navette-cut diamonds the leaves and petals, centered by a 23.6-carat rose-pink diamond. It was presented as a wedding gift to the queen by the Canadian geologist John T. Williamson. Her Majesty is wearing it in the photograph with her daughter, Princess Anne.

Below: The diamond-set rose blossom brooch by David Webb was made in the 1960s.

Right: Germaine Boivin designed this
cedar tree brooch for her mother, Jeanne
Boivin's, 80th birthday in 1951. It is a com-
memorative family tree for the René
Boivin company. Not only are the firm's
traditions evident in the use of colored
gemstones including pink tourmalines,
amethysts, and green garnets, but the tree
is also cleverly fitted with a series of folding plaques engraved with the names of
designers, master jewelers, and associates
who worked closely with the company.
Bottom: In the mid 1950s, Julius Cohen
designed this gold weeping willow brooch
with dangling peridots to represent the
leaves. Diamond accents highlight the
branches and roots. Below: Julius Cohen
designed this flower-pot brooch with
leaves of round and marquise diamonds
with a pear-shape diamond at the top
while the flower pot is an unusual 4.15-
carat portrait diamond. This brooch was
exhibited in the 1957 Diamonds International Awards where it won a prize for
excellence of design.

The palm tree continued to be popular in the late 1950s, as seen in the following two examples in which the palm fronds and trunk are set with circular-cut and baguette-cut diamonds. The Cartier tree (left) was made in 1957 on a special order in Paris. The coconuts are seven cushion-shape Burmese rubies weighing 23.10 carats. The Bulgari tree (below), made in France, c. 1960, is accented with marquise-cut diamonds while the coconuts are vari-cut sapphires.

These three examples of flower-pot brooches were made by Bulgari during the 1960s. Known as *giardinetto* brooches, the flower vases are made of cabochon sapphires or rubies from which sprays of diamond and multicolored gemstone flowers emerge.

Opposite: The original Parisian jeweler's design from Maison Duhem shows eleven examples.

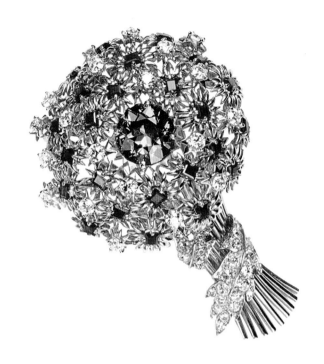

The bouquet, especially of violets, was a popular jeweled form during the early 1960s. Small pear-shaped amethysts form the petals with ruby centers while the leaves are set with demantoid garnets on a bouquet of violets by René Boivin (opposite). A violet corsage by Fulco di Verdura is set with amethysts, diamonds, and cabochon emeralds (below). Large oval and pear-shape amethysts combine to form a violet bouquet with peridot leaves by René Boivin from 1962 (below left). Tiffany & Co. created an unusual bouquet in platinum and gold with rubies and diamonds and a fancy yellow-brown diamond at the center (left).

Opposite: This suite, by Jean Schlumberger for Tiffany & Co., was a special order in 1960 with the customer's Colombian emeralds. The leaves are pavé diamonds.

These foliate jewels were designed by Jean Schlumberger for Tiffany & Co. In this popular pair of pavé-diamond earrings (right), first made in 1955, the leaves appear to pierce the ears. The bracelet (middle) with black and white pearls and pavé-diamond leaves is formed with branches and stems in 18K gold and dates to 1964. The matching earrings (bottom), which are set with natural pearls, date to 1966.

Right: Donald Claflin, one of Tiffany & Co.'s most innovative designers, was the creator of this bracelet depicting strawberries in coral with gold achenes, diamond-set flowers, and leaves of diamonds and enamel, 1968. Below right: A ruby brooch depicting a strawberry, with leaves of marquise-shaped diamonds, designed by Jean Schlumberger for Tiffany & Co., was first introduced in 1957. This brooch dates to 1961. Below: This brooch in the form of a watermelon slice uses graduated shades of rubies for the fruit and marquise-shape sapphires for the seeds. It was made by the Parisian jeweler Marchak in the mid 1950s.

Below: An interesting brooch, designed by Donald Claflin for Tiffany & Co. in the late 1960s, is a cherry branch freshly picked from the tree with coral cherries and diamond-set leaves. Below left: A gold, emerald, and diamond pineapple brooch by Tiffany & Co., France, was made in the 1960s. Left: Fulco di Verdura designed this pomegranate brooch during the 1950s in peridots with cabochon rubies to depict the luscious interior fruit. Yellow diamonds highlight the top of the flower head and stem of the fruit. The earrings were made by Verdura on special order in the early 1990s.

Right: Pierre Sterlé made this thistle brooch in multicolored tourmalines and diamonds in 1967. Bottom: This thistle brooch by Verdura was made with sapphire flowers, accented with diamonds, and a cabochon emerald.

Opposite left: In 1957, Jean Schlumberger for Tiffany & Co. created a special brooch for Amory Houghton using the customer's jade pea pods with leaves of olivines and diamonds. Opposite right: This wisteria brooch, upon which a diamond-set butterfly is perched, is by Marchak, c. 1955. The entire brooch is *en tremblant*, meaning that the pear- and marquise-shape sapphires and round emeralds flowers move when worn.

Opposite: A platinum and diamond necklace by Van Cleef & Arpels from 1954 depicts a wheat sheaf in round and pear-shape diamonds.

Left: This white-lilacs brooch was designed by Fulco di Verdura as a flexible, cascading cluster of lilac, set with twenty-one pear-shape diamonds and twenty-nine round diamonds. It has a curling leaf and a curving branch. Below: David Webb made the bracelet depicting grapes and grape vines in cabochon emeralds and diamonds in the 1960s.

Right: A cornucopia brooch formed out of a 59-carat natural abalone pearl is abundantly filled with fruits and flowers in diamonds, white and black natural pearls, conch pearls, and engraved emeralds. It was made in Scotland in the 1950s. Below right: A brooch by Marc Koven of a flower head is artfully created. A cabochon coral is set into the center, which appears to be an enameled Renaissance jewel with one diamond-set leaf. Below: This three-piece suite of brooch and pair of earrings was made by the Beverly Hills jeweler William Ruser in the late 1950s. It is made with freshwater pearls and diamonds.

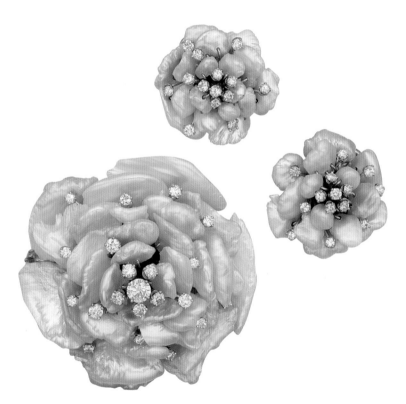

This stylized dahlia by Pierre Sterlé dates to 1964. The petals are made from mother-of-pearl while the center is made of gold fringe. The stem is made of pavé diamonds set in platinum, finished off with baguettes to emphasize the twist in the stem. Toledo Museum of Art.

Right: Sketches from the Verdura archives represent the variety of botanical jewels he designed. Included in this group is an unusual ear of corn with black pearl kernels. Below: With a whimsical touch, Verdura designed these brooches of enameled pixies taking shelter under diamond-set mushrooms.

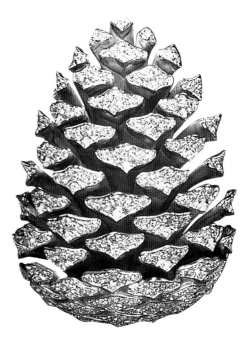

Below: Fulco di Verdura first introduced the gold and pavé diamond pine cone brooch at the beginning of the 1950s. Bottom: A design drawing for a holly-leaf and berry bracelet by Oscar Heyman & Brothers dates to 1968. Left: A design drawing for a Christmas tree brooch by Maison Duhem, Parisian fabricators for Bulgari dates to the early 1960s.

This orchid brooch from c. 1960 in yellow
and near-colorless diamonds was made by
Ghiso, a jewelry firm established in Buenos
Aires in the late nineteenth century,
which later had locations in New York and
Paris. Oscar Ghiso, son of the founder,
designed this orchid in the actual size and
floral structure of the flower. He liked this
brooch so much that he presented it to
his second wife, Contessa Daria, upon
their marriage in 1978.

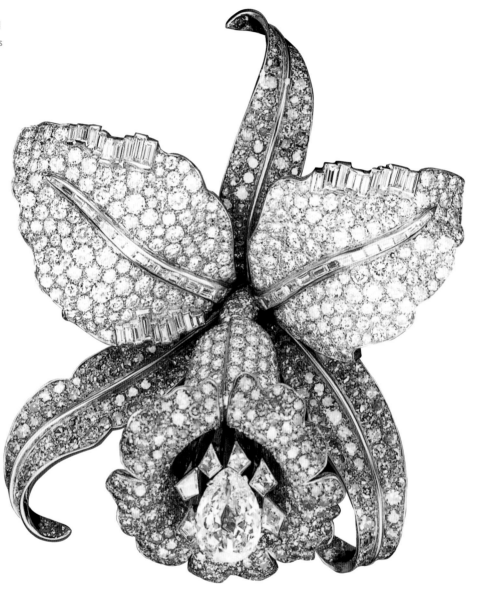

CHAPTER SIX

The Seventies to the Present

Individual Designers Develop Distinctive Styles

The period from the 1970s through the turn of the twenty-first century witnessed a time of relative stability. A serious oil crisis was eventually resolved and no major threats to world peace flared up as international conflicts remained confined to relatively small geographic areas, mostly in the Middle East. The cold war that had been ongoing since the 1950s came to an end in 1991 with communism no longer playing a major economic role. The world was rapidly changing from insular nations concerned primarily with their own economic growth to a global economy. In 1993, twelve European nations founded the European Union to enhance political, economic, and social cooperation; thirteen other countries joined at later dates. In the world of finance, a new breed of investment emerged, the hedge fund, and the Dow Jones index first broke the 10,000 mark on March 29, 1999.

This time of prosperity produced great wealth not only in the financial world but also in other areas such as entertainment, where leading actors and actresses were paid in the multiple millions for a single movie performance and top professional athletes earned tens of millions of dollars for just one season of play. Millionaire status no longer held the cachet it once enjoyed with the emergence of highly publicized billionaires, such as Ted Turner of Turner Enterprises and Bill Gates of Microsoft. In this new environment, the art world, whose major patronage had been primarily among private collectors, became an area with significant investment potential for businesses assembling corporate collections.

All of this impacted the jewelry industry, however indirectly, resulting in more emphasis on marketing as well as the promotion of new products—such as leather goods and perfume—than on innovative design.

Below: The flower brooch by David Webb, c. 1970, is a fine example of a beautiful bloom with textured gold petals accented with diamond-set curled tips, pear-shape diamond pistils, and a baguette-set diamond stem. It was made on special commission with the customer's stones after one of the firm's classic designs. Bottom: A gold and diamond bracelet by Harry Winston is composed of flower heads joined by foliate sprigs, c.1970.

The major jewelry houses of Cartier, Van Cleef & Arpels, Bulgari, and Tiffany & Co. still created beautiful jewelry but the design impetus shifted to individual designers, many of whom did not maintain their own salons, preferring to offer their jewelry through fine retailers such as Neiman Marcus, Saks Fifth Avenue, or Bergdorf Goodman.

Beginning in the 1980s, the auction houses, which heretofore had been a source primarily for the trade, began to promote jewelry to the private sector. With the sale of the Duchess of Windsor's jewelry on April 2 and 3, 1987 and, nine years later, that of Jacqueline Kennedy Onassis's jewelry on April 24 and 25, 1996, the public began buying jewelry at auction, driving prices far beyond their estimates. In the 1990s, contemporary jewelers were featured in their sales[1] and, in 2002, Sotheby's opened Salon Privé, a private-sales department offering fine jewelry which, in 2005, became Sotheby's Diamonds.

What the public wanted was beautiful, well-designed jewelry, something out of the ordinary, and they were willing to pay for it. Many saw the acquisition of fine jewels as a wealth protector, a hedge against a somewhat fickle stock market. A new group of designers arose to satisfy this demand, creating a plethora of new designs in keeping with the times.

The impetus towards a new design direction, which began in the 1970s, is a reflection of the Minimalist art movement of the 1960s that affected jewelry design in the following decade. The stripped-down-elemental, geometric forms, presented in an impersonal manner were characteristic of the sculptures of Donald Judd and Sol LeWitt and the paintings of Ellsworth Kelly and Frank Stella. In jewelry, this was interpreted by eliminating extraneous details, with little or no ornamentation, and by using nontraditional jewelry material. In 1970, Cartier designed a brooch and matching ear clips of just daisy flowerheads without any leaves or stems and whose petals are carved out of an exotic wood instead of gold or platinum (opposite, top). Two years later, Van Cleef & Arpels adopted this concept on a set of clematis jewelry made from amourette wood (opposite, bottom).

Left: These flower head brooch and earrings by Cartier, Paris were made out of an exotic wood with gold centers set with diamonds, 1970. Below: In 1972, Van Cleef & Arpels created a clematis brooch and earrings out of amourette wood. The centers of the flowers are set with diamonds.

Below: Paloma Picasso designed this pair
of hardstone and peridot leaf earrings for
Tiffany & Co. in 1983.

Opposite: Angela Cummings designed this
necklace and ear clips for Tiffany & Co.
in 1979. It is composed of a series of gold
rose petals.

Angela Cummings, who started working at Tiffany & Co. in 1967 as Donald Claflin's assistant, had her first line introduced by the company in 1973. She became known for her unusual combinations of materials and for her nature-inspired designs. Her minimalist vision is exemplified by a necklace and earrings where instead of depicting an entire rose blossom, she displays only individual flower petals, each looking as if a real one were dipped in gold (opposite). This necklace was featured in the firm's 1979 annual catalogue where it was described as "rose petal necklace of hand-hammered eighteen karat yellow gold with red gold highlights."[2]

Cummings left Tiffany's in 1984, forming her own company in partnership with her husband, Bruce, offering her jewelry through fine retailers such as Bergdorf Goodman, Saks Fifth Avenue, and Neiman Marcus in the United States as well as at Takashimaya and Shiseido in Japan. She continued to design jewelry with botanical motifs but in an atypical way, creating a necklace and earrings out of matte gold and red, yellow, brown, and orange enameled sunflowers, some shown in their entirety while others overlap their neighbors, partially obscuring the bloom (p. 172). Again, details on the blossoms are significantly simplified.

David Webb, who is best known for his patterned necklaces and his enameled animal jewelry of the 1960s, created a line of porcelain flower jewelry in the late 1950s to complement the fashion designs of Christian Dior and Marcel Rochas. He also made flower jewelry set with fine diamonds, such as a bloom in which round diamonds accent the tips of the petals with pear shapes at the center and baguettes for the stem (p. 168).

The venerable firm of Harry Winston has consistently made jewelry with the finest diamonds, the gemstone for which the firm is noted. Winston revolutionized diamond jewelry design by reinterpreting the relationship of gemstones and their mountings. Above all, he wanted to showcase diamonds, letting them dictate the design. To achieve this, his designers devised a new mounting that featured flexible wire settings that held stones in place without upstaging them. That was a perfect setting for floral jewelry in which the diamonds formed the entire design with no visible mounting showing, as epitomized in their iconic wreath necklace that is based on a floral wreath, with diamonds layered to give depth and dimension (p. 202). A pair of floral earrings in which diamonds portray the petals and a pink diamond the center also underscores the importance Winston attached to these stones (p. 184).

Oscar Heyman continued to make beautiful floral jewelry, deriving inspiration for their designs from simple flowers such as the lily of the valley, a flower that they first introduced in 1938. In this case, instead of depicting an entire bouquet, they chose just one section with two leaves, enameled dark green as found in nature, with diamond-set stems from which spring the bell-shaped flowers, here shown as nine pearls, a slight variation from the design drawing, which shows only eight (p. 177). The orchid is another example of an adaptation from 1936 in which the labellum is now

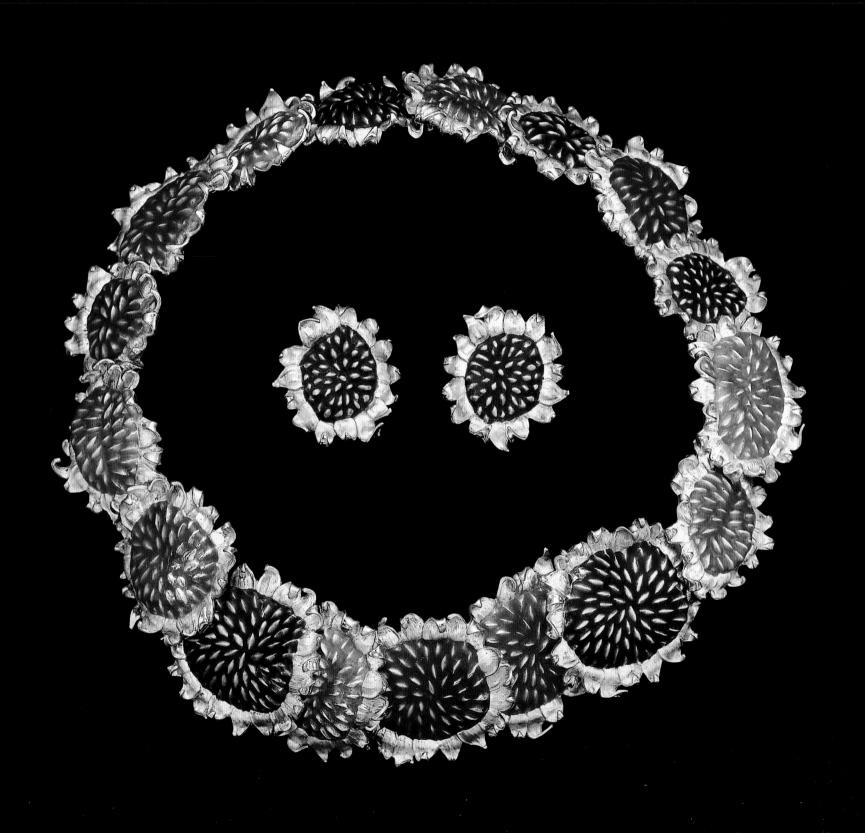

set with yellow and white diamonds instead of enameling it (p. 182). A novel addition to their botanical repertoire is the pussy willow with pavé diamonds making up the flowers (p. 177).

The designers who emerged in the 1990s and after the turn of the twenty-first century were a new breed who did look to the past for inspiration and translated that knowledge into fresh, exciting jewels. Traditionally, jewelry design centers had been located in metropolitan areas such as New York and Paris. In this later period, while these cities continued to play a role, many of the new designers were situated in other areas.

Neil Lane, from Los Angeles, began in the jewelry business offering antique jewelry before designing his own line with flowers and leaves, including a bangle bracelet with three flowers, each one set in either white, yellow, or pink diamonds. Lane is perhaps best known for his diamond rings, many of which have been purchased by movie stars. In 2004, he designed a line of rings with botanical motifs, including one with leaves forming the mounting (p. 184). Martin Katz from the same city also got his start in the antique jewelry business. He has created a variety of botanically inspired jewelry, including a strawberry brooch, leaf brooch, ivy necklace, and an inventive tulip brooch with interchangeable flowerheads (p. 194). He also updated the grape-bunch theme, using tsavorite garnets for the leaves and twenty-five old rose-cut diamonds for the grapes (p. 186).

Michelle Ong, located in Hong Kong, sells under the name Carnet. She is very particular about her designs, taking an extraordinary amount of time with each of her botanical-inspired creations but the end result is always a jewel that projects the visual impact that nature intended. On a pair of ear pendants, briolette-cut diamond grapes dangle like the fruit on the vine. Her preference for strong color contrasts is evident: white diamond grapes for one bunch and black diamonds for the other with the corresponding leaves also in opposite colorations (p. 186).

Joel Arthur Rosenthal, known simply as JAR, offers his jewels out of his Paris boutique at 7 Place Vendôme. He looks to the past for inspiration, utilizing techniques from the nineteenth century but updating them to the present. Conscious of the subtleties driving jewelry design, he strives for the perfect effect, whether it is the choice of gemstones or the metal into which they are set, always with meticulous attention to detail. In the nineteenth century, diamonds were set into silver that, over time, oxidized. JAR took this idea a step further, transforming a conventional-style bangle bracelet into a work of art by utilizing oxidized titanium, an iridescent metal with color change, as the base metal for the floral design on the Moghul Flower bracelet (p. 188). The gemstones composing the flowers are set in the pavé style to simulate the imagery prevalent in Indian art and textiles. Penny Proddow and Marion Fasel noted, "To create the lack of perspective or flat appearance of the buds and blooms in Indian work, Rosenthal set evenly matched selections of rubies, diamonds, sapphires, and amethysts in silver."[3]

For the past two decades, New York has been the principal center for jewelry design, where many talented designers reinterpret the past while also creating jewelry for the new millennium.

Opposite: The necklace and earrings by Angela Cummings designed as overlapping matte-finished and polished gold sunflowers with enameled centers was made in 1993.

Below: Design drawings from the Boucheron archives, 1974 and 1975, depict gem-set floral brooches.

Right: A design drawing for a necklace by Maison Duhem for Bulgari depicts lotus leaves in cabochon sapphires, coral, and onyx. It dates to about 1980. Below: A design drawing for a floral pendant necklace in gold, amethysts, citrines, and turquoise by Maison Duhem for Bulgari dates to c.1970.

In 2004, Bulgari presented this stunning floral necklace with flower petals made out of pear-shape violet, pink, blue and yellow, sapphires, each accented with baguette diamonds and an emerald. Diamond-set gold ring configurations, each set with a pearl, diamond, and emerald, unites the design.

Right: This corsage brooch of a spray of flowers with a bee hovering nearby was designed in 2000 by Ella Gafter for Ellagem. It is made out of platinum with Australian South Sea pearls, diamonds, rock crystal, and yellow sapphires. Below: In 1993, the Parisian couture house Chanel introduced a new line of jewelry featuring cacholong, a stone that looks like porcelain. In these camellia rings the white is sculpted from cacholong while the black is sculpted from onyx.

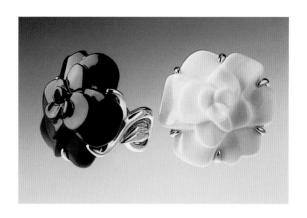

Below: This pussy-willow brooch was designed by Edmond Chin in 2002. The stems are pavé-set with brown diamonds, while the catkins are peridots. Left: Two additions to the Oscar Heyman & Brothers repertoire of jewelry designs include a pussy-willow brooch with textured gold stem and pavé diamond catkins from 1997 (left) and the lily-of-the-valley brooch in diamonds, pearls, and green enamel from 1993 (far left). The latter is accompanied by its original drawing.

HEYMAN & BROTHERS

Right: The poppy-flower brooch was created by Stefan Hemmerle in 1994. The petals are formed with fancy-shape rubies, the pistil and anther with colored diamonds, and the calyx and removable stem with tsavorites. Bottom right: The basket of pansies was created by Stefan Hemmerle in 1996. Realizing that flowers are not one solid color, he utilized sapphires and aquamarines to achieve the graduation in colors on the flower petals. The basket is a rectangular scissor-cut aquamarine.

Those that contributed imaginative botanically inspired jewelry include Christopher Walling, Marilyn Cooperman, Henry Dunay, Ella Gafter, James de Givenchy, and Sorab Bouzarjomehri.

Christopher Walling looked to the Russian past for inspiration for his pair of quince blossom ear clips (p. 190, left). The arrangement of the blossoms is reminiscent of flower spray brooches designed by Duval for Catherine the Great, while the use of opposite or contrasting motifs is contemporary. Drawing inspiration from real-life specimens, he depicted the flowers at the moment the blossom is picked from the stem, with leaves curling around the buds in various stages of opening, a theme also seen in Art Nouveau jewelry. He set the flowers with pink diamonds from the Argyle mines in Australia and the leaves with demantoid garnets. Many years after designing the quince blossom ear clips, Walling created a brooch in the form of an Aspen leaf with pink sapphires surrounding a cushion-cut Siberian amethyst in the center (p. 190, right).

Leaves from a tree she saw while relaxing poolside in Boca Raton inspired Marilyn Cooperman's Boca brooch. She was so excited by the exotic-looking leaves that she pressed them for future study, eventually creating jewelry versions of them in several different sizes arranged into a spiny brooch with carved citrines (p. 180). She also readapted the ever present ivy necklace concept with leaves of various sizes and shapes in patinated silver that have been engraved for texture, accented with Ceylon moonstones denoting dew drops. She fashioned the connecting twigs out of a specially designed warm-colored gold instead of the usual yellow or green tones (p. 181).

South Sea pearls are the trademark gem for Ella Gafter, who offers her jewelry under the trade name Ellagem. She is renowned for her ability to select just the right pearl with just the right luminescence, as on a corsage ornament where pearls make up the centers of the flowers (p. 176). The leaves are either pavé-set with diamonds or fashioned out of frosted rock crystal, and some are highlighted with diamonds on the edge or tip of the leaf as it curls around. This subtlety provides movement within the design. This elegant brooch was featured in the ground-breaking exhibition *Pearls: A Natural History*, at the American Museum of Natural History in New York and the Field Museum in Chicago.

When Henry Dunay designs a botanical jewel, it is expected to be out of the ordinary. Instead of choosing just another garden flower, like the rose or pansy, he looked to the East, creating Japanese bonsai-tree brooches with appropriately shaped diamonds for leaves, replicating miniature specimens growing in pots. His three examples reproduce different varieties of bonsai, all in his signature 18-karat gold Sabi finish: the *moyogi* with its graceful turns in the trunk; the *kengai* with its characteristic bent trunk and low-hanging branches; and the *shidare* or *zukuri* with its weeping-style branches (p. 192).

Sorab Bouzarjomehri and his wife, Roshi Ameri, formed Sorab & Roshi, specializing in one-of-a-kind jewels, all hand-crafted by Sorab. His creative combinations of unusual materials, such as shells, bone, wood, abalone, carved gemstones, and baroque pearls with precious and colored gem-

Below: This diamond and ruby *ombelle* or Queen Anne's Lace brooch by René Boivin is a 1990s revival of an earlier design. Diamond florettes mounted in platinum and 18K gold are set *en tremblant* and surround a ruby center over a baguette diamond stem.

Right: The first radish brooch by René Boivin was made in 1985, using rhodocrosite for the vegetable. When it was made a few years later, coral was the stone of choice for the radishes accented with diamonds and with periodot leaves on this brooch. Below right: New York designer Marilyn Cooperman named this jewel *Boca Brooch* after leaves fallen from a tree in Boca Raton, Florida. The gold spiny leaves with diamond veins surround carved citrines, 1997. Below: Joel Arthur Rosenthal of JAR, Paris, readapted the oak theme on a pair of pendant ear clips with the tops styled as leaves with acorns of bluish-gray banded agate.

Marilyn Cooperman readapted the ivy
necklace in 2003 with leaves in patinated
silver, engraved for texture, and with
gold veins. Ceylon moonstones serve as
dew drops.

Oscar Heyman & Brothers first introduced the orchid design into their repertoire in 1936. It remains a favorite, now made with yellow and white diamonds with green enameled leaves.

stones, gives his jewelry a flair that is uniquely his own. His work exhibits a wonderful sense of color, balance, and proportion, as epitomized by a chrysanthemum brooch where matching fresh-water pearls make up the petals around a ruby core whose deep reddish hue presents an artful contrast to the supporting coral branch (p. 190).

Color is also important to James de Givenchy who began designing jewelry in 1996 under the Taffin name. He is always looking for that interesting, underutilized colorful gemstone. "I'm crazy about spinels," says de Givenchy. "They are a true red, extremely rare, and still largely undiscovered by clients."[4] He uses them in novel contexts such as for flowers on a cactus whose simple lines allow full attention to be focused on the chromatic composition (p. 193). His floral repertoire includes blooms that are not specific to any natural flower. Rather, they are generalizations using the blossom as a vehicle to create a jewel with three-dimensionality, with volume. One flower is made up of seven spessartite garnets that encircle the center stone with coral beads, each set with

a diamond, demarcating the boundary. Alternating pink sapphires and old mine-cut diamonds line the outer edge of the flower (p. 190). He also created a special brooch in honor of the one hundred fiftieth anniversary of New York's Central Park in 2005. The trunk is engraved with markings to replicate the bark while the leaves are sculpted tourmalines (p. 193).

In Munich, Stefan Hemmerle has been changing the "look" of fine jewelry, preferring the term, "New Objectivity," to describe his minimalist style. In his words, "I want to tread a middle path between the decorative arts and the severe. I wanted my clients to feel that they have found someone who can bring essentials to the fore— but with imagination!"[5] Following this path, one of his specialties is to represent simple botanical motifs drawn from the natural world. A fern frond is depicted naturalistically in a gentle "S" shape with the feathery divisions of the leaf set irregularly (p. 195). The flowerhead of a calla lily is set with white and pink diamonds, while the spadix is formed with a 27.82-carat conch pearl. A remarkable detail of this exquisitely crafted flower is the setting of the diamonds on the back of the spathe; not on the front side but on the back side with the culets protruding through to the front, giving an unusual look as well as feel to the piece (p. 195).

The inspiration for Hemmerle's perhaps most inventive botanical jewels came to him one day while he was sitting with his niece who was perusing a scientific book in which he spied a page with mushrooms. Shortly afterwards, he designed the first of a series of brooches on this theme with the initial group including a generic mushroom, a chanterelle and a morel (p. 196). The following year, he created more exotic species of *Rhodophyllus clypaetus*, *Russula virescens*, and *Cortinarius sanguineus*, each with bits of dirt at the bottom of the stem. The caps of the latter three are fashioned either out of wood, bronze, or are set with sapphires (p. 197).

In the 1980s, the Parisian house of Boivin was once again making imaginative and unexpected jewels following the precepts of Jeanne Boivin. Who would ever have thought that the humble radish would inspire an attractive jewel! But that is exactly what this time-honored firm succeeded in doing. Their brooch is designed as a cluster of coral radishes, each enhanced with diamonds to denote the roots, crowned by gold leaves set with peridots. A diamond-set ribbon holds the bunch together (p. 180).

The Parisian couture house Chanel has re-created their signature flower, the camellia, in a variety of materials including precious gemstones as well as cacholong, a stone that looks like porcelain.[6] They chose this stone for its similarity to the porcelain jewelry Coco Chanel made in the late 1930s, which was featured in an editorial in a 1938 issue of *Harper's Bazaar*.[7] Cacholong is also the main stone in necklaces, rings, and earrings (p. 176).

Gianmaria Buccellati continues the tradition of his father, Mario, making beautiful jewelry with their trademark gold work, especially those with floral representations. Sculpted roses decorate a pendant brooch, using pink gold for the flowers and yellow gold for the leaves and stems, all finished

Beginning in 1977, Angela Cummings began designing jewelry inlaid with hand-carved hardstones for Tiffany & Co. She created these ear clips around 1980, in the guise of orchids abstracted into two dimensions, inlaid with opal, mother-of-pearl, and onyx.

in the firm's characteristic engraving techniques. A large conch pearl completes the elegant color scheme (p. 208). Flower petals on a mountain thistle brooch are set with white and yellow diamonds with rose-cut diamonds set into the gold pinnatifid leaves, finished with veins engraved into the surface. A chromo tourmaline makes up the center of the flowerhead. The liveliness of the flower is captured in the dynamic shaping of the leaves and the petals (p. 208).

The flower is interpreted in a very different way on a line of Asprey jewelry based on the jacaranda, the large flowering tropical tree found in California and Australia. For a bracelet, they fitted the simple, smooth shapes of the leaves into stylized diamond-set forms (p. 185).

The late 1990s through the beginning of the twentieth century saw a revival of important, even sumptuous, necklaces ornamented with flowers. These necklaces are in the spirit of some of the great examples from the nineteenth century and the Edwardian period. It seems designers again felt free to capture the flower in all its grandeur and in unusual ways.

The hardstone sculptor Andreas von Zadora-Gerlof from New York and London, who is known for his realistic carvings of animals as well as for his unusual clocks and other objects that move, translates the world of flora into jewelry that is at once attractive to look at and lovely to wear. Although sculpting gemstone flowers is a European tradition that dates back to the Renaissance and Baroque periods, the best-known examples of this art are those executed by the Fabergé workshop in Russia in the late 1800s. Zadora took these depictions one step further, creating necklaces that look like wreaths that wrap around a woman's neck as if the branches, leaves, and flowers were natural, as epitomized by the necklace with rhododendron blossoms and leaves. The rhododendrons are sculpted in pink tourmaline from Maine with diamond-set pistils and stamens, watermelon tourmaline buds, and green tourmaline leaves. The flowers are set *en tremblant* so they quiver when the necklace is worn (p. 200).

In Geneva, Michele Della Valle created a floral-inspired necklace with unusual color hues. At the center of each flowerhead, an oval ruby is nested onto four diamond-set petals that, in turn, are nested onto a five-petal ensemble set with color-change garnets. Ruby buds and leaves set with green garnets complete the design. The somewhat muted color palette, not as bright as would be the case if precious gemstones were used, instead draws attention to the dramatic effect of the entire ensemble (p. 201).

In a banner year for fine jewelry, 2005, several jewelry houses launched new collections based on botanical imagery with fresh, novel ideas, pointing to a new direction in design for the new millennium. These collections included important necklaces in the spirit of great pieces from the past, when jewelry design was more than just about beautiful gemstones but instead emphasizing the creative impulse, the making of something without the constraints of the marketplace: in essence, creating jewelry for its sheer beauty.

Left: The pear-shape Montana sapphires on this necklace form a wreath, beginning with a five-petal flower from which emanates a series of two petals that encircle the neck. It was designed in the early 1970s by Stanley Kazanjian for Kazanjian Brothers, Beverly Hills. Below: In 2003, Asprey created a novel bracelet based on the jacaranda, a large flowering tropical tree in California and Australia, using each leaf, diamond-set in platinum, in a series of two or three as it wraps around the wrist.

Below: These ear pendants in the form of grape bunches were made in 2003 by Michelle Ong for Carnet, Hong Kong. The grapes are formed with briolette-cut diamonds, one bunch in white diamonds and the other in black diamonds with the leaves in the opposite color schemes. Below right: In 2001, Van Cleef & Arpels reintroduced the invisibly-set grape leaf with emeralds, a stone that, with advancements in cutting technology, can now be shaped into the desired cuts for this difficult technique. Right: In the early 2000s, Martin Katz of Los Angeles created a grape bunch-brooch with tsavorite garnets for the leaves and rose-cut diamonds for the grapes. The stems are pavé-set diamonds.

Bulgari introduced a line of jewelry with fancy color sapphires forming blossoms. The subtlety of the colorations is most pronounced on a necklace where the petals of most of the flowers feature sapphires of various colors, each accented with baguette diamonds and an emerald. Connecting diamond-set gold ring configurations, each accented with a pearl, emeralds, and diamonds, tie the design together (p. 175).

Cartier's designer Jacqueline Karachi-Langane, who oversees the firm's *haute joaillerie* studio, was inspired by a hair comb in the company's archives, as well as by nature itself, for a special collection of jewelry with orchid motifs. Her interpretation is quite different from Tiffany's enameled confections from 1889 or Boivin's diamond-and-ruby orchid from 1936. For the centerpiece of a necklace, Karachi-Langane chose a chromatically simpler, more luxurious orchid with curling sepals set with diamonds and rubies and an 18.40-carat faceted rubellite at the center. It is set amidst sumptuous emeralds and rubellites, with diamonds serving as dewdrops (p. 207).

Victoire de Castellane has been designing jewelry for Christian Dior since they ventured into this field in 1998. She has been quoted as saying that she "likes things that are exaggerated. Big, comic-book–style jewelry, because jewelry is only beautiful if you take notice of it."[8] True to that credo, her special collection with fruits and vegetables is sure to capture attention when worn. The inspiration for this new group, known as Milly La Forêt, came from Christian Dior's country house, where he loved to work in the garden. On a necklace, the designer incorporated a colorful collage of assorted fruits and vegetables such as cherries, radishes, pea pods, and raspberries, which, though unusual, present a pleasantly harmonious image (p. 206).

While the new millennium brought new ideas and new concepts into jewelry design, it also saw a resurgence of techniques that have been dormant for many years. Laura Hiserote, working out of her studio in Vancouver, Washington, has created some of the most spectacular micromosaics, using extremely fine tesserae to differentiate the subtle color tones for the datura blossom and leaves (p. 209).[9] David Freda from San Clemente, California has been making enameled orchids in the spirit of Paulding Farnham's flowers for Tiffany & Co. For each piece, he dips a live orchid into hot wax to create a form for a 20-karat gold brooch, which he then enamels in colors true to each species. His orchids project the dynamic quality of live specimens, which he further enhances by accenting with diamond-set dew drops (p. 209).

Over the past two hundred years, the evolution of botanical imagery in jewelry design has run the gamut from revival styles to truly innovative one-of-a-kind designs; from the mundane to the splendiferous; from stylizations to realistic depictions. In so doing, it utilized a plethora of botanical motifs, many of which had originated at almost the beginning of civilization. It all adds up to a rich and beautiful jewelry tradition, one that will continue to fascinate both designers and wearers of the jewelry.

A pair of chili-pepper ear pendants by the Geneva jeweler Michele della Valle are made with coral peppers with a stem of green garnets set into 18-karat white gold.

tinted titanium and decorated with
undulating blossoms of rubies, sapphires,
diamonds, and amethysts, with tsavorite
garnet with tourmaline stems, 1987.

Opposite: Seven Moghul flower brooches
from 1987 by JAR, all center on relatively
important stones of an emerald, a
paparadscha sapphire, a ruby, a pink topaz,
a yellow diamond, a white diamond, and
a spinel. The petals and stems are set with
rubies, amethysts, tourmalines, garnets,
and yellow and white diamonds.

Top: A chrysanthemum brooch by Sorab Bouzarjomehri of Sorab & Roshi is made up of freshwater pearl petals with a ruby at the center and a coral branch. It was made in 2005. Far right: Christopher Walling of New York turned to one of his favorite vacation spots, Aspen, Colorado, for the imagery for this aspen-leaf brooch from 2004. The center stone is a cushion-cut Siberian amethyst, surrounded by pink sapphires with a diamond stem. Near right: In 2005, James de Givenchy for Taffin, New York, created a flower brooch with spessartite garnets, coral accented with diamonds, and pink sapphires. Below: Christopher Walling created a pair of quince blossom earrings in 1991. The flowers are set with pink diamonds, leaves with demantoid garnets and stems with diamonds.

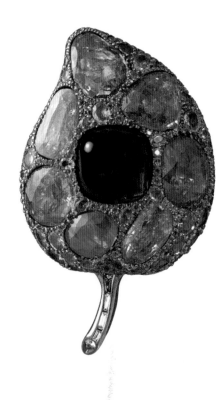

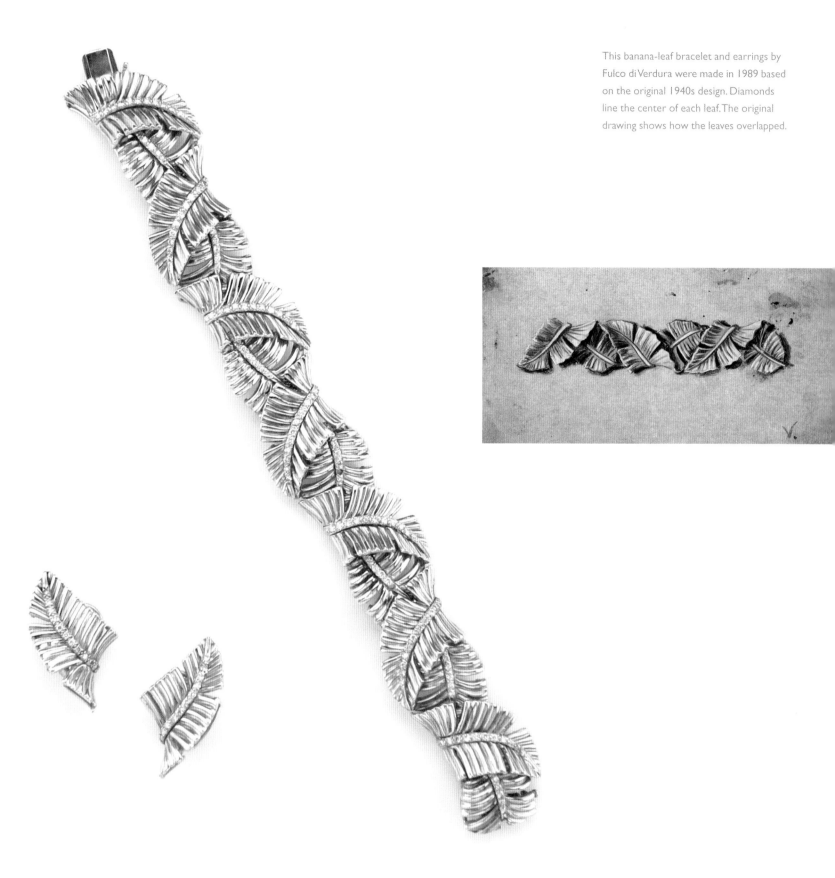

This banana-leaf bracelet and earrings by Fulco di Verdura were made in 1989 based on the original 1940s design. Diamonds line the center of each leaf. The original drawing shows how the leaves overlapped.

Opposite: Three Japanese bonsai tree brooches by Henry Dunay include the kengai (upper right), moyogi (middle), and shidare or zukuri (bottom). Each is crafted in 18-karat gold Sabi finish with the leaves of diamonds.

Left: James de Givenchy for Taffin created a special tree brooch of gold and tourmalines to commemorate the 150th anniversary of Central Park, New York, in 2005. Below: The unusual captivates James de Givenchy, who designed two brooches as cacti in cabochon emeralds, set with spinels for the flowers, growing out of jasper pots.

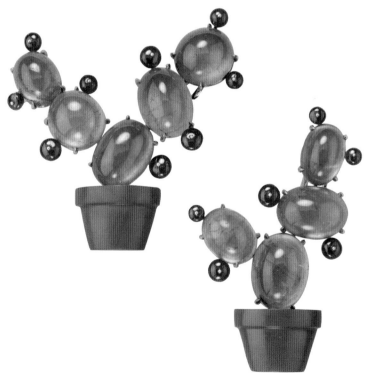

Right: A tulip brooch by Martin Katz of Beverly Hills is pavé-set with pink sapphires, amethysts, and diamonds, while tsavorite garnets make up the stem and leaves which are trimmed in diamonds. The flower head is interchangeable with other gem-set versions. Below: In 1992, Christopher Walling designed these tulip ear clips that convert to clip brooches. They were made by Carvin French. The flower heads are pavé-set diamonds, the stems in baguette diamonds, and the leaves in sapphires.

In 2004, Stefan Hemmerle created a fern-frond brooch with green sapphires, diamonds, white gold, and silver. The next year he designed a calla-lily brooch with flower head set with white and pink diamonds, the spadix with a 27.82-carat conch pearl, while demantoid garnets make up the stem.

In 2004, Stefan Hemmerle created the
first three of his mushroom brooches.
They are the chanterelle in gold (top), the
morel in white gold (bottom right), and
another mushroom in white gold, silver,
and sapphires (bottom left).

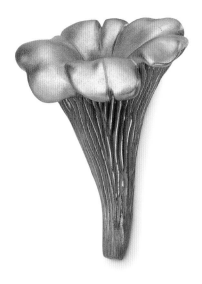

Stefan Hemmerle continued the mushroom theme in 2005, making the *Rhodophyllus clypeatus* in white gold, copper, and wood (left); *Cortinarius sanguineus* in pink gold, copper, and sapphires (bottom right); and *Russula virescens* in white gold, silver, and bronze.

In the 1990s, Oscar Heyman & Brothers introduced brooches with Christmas imagery, including a Christmas tree set with sapphires, rubies, emeralds, and diamonds in 1991, shown with its original drawing (right); a poinsettia with rubies and diamonds in 1993 (below); and a wreath with rubies, emeralds, and diamonds in 1994 (bottom right).

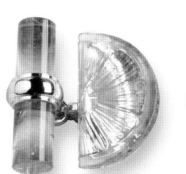 

Left: Three pairs of cufflinks depicting fruit: strawberries in coral, lemon slices in yellow beryl, and pineapples in citrine quartz with tourmaline rosettes of thick spiny leaves were made by Villa Gioielliere, c. 2000. Below: This strawberry brooch made in oval cabochon rubies with pavé-set diamond flowers and green emerald leaves was made in 1995 by Oscar Heyman & Brothers.

Opposite: The rhododendron necklace by Andreas von Zadora-Gerlof from 1994 is made with pink tourmaline blossoms, watermelon tourmaline buds, green tourmaline leaves, and diamond pistils and stamens. A yellow and white diamond-set bee, pollinating the flowers, functions as the clasp.

Left: A floral necklace and earrings by Michele della Valle, c. 2000, is made with flower heads of pavé-set diamonds and color-change garnets surrounding ruby centers. The leaves are pavé-set green garnets.

Opposite: The iconic Harry Winston jewel is the wreath necklace with diamonds layered to give depth and dimension. This necklace is set with a total of 120 carats of diamonds.

Right: Revisiting the flower-basket theme is this brooch from New York jeweler Carvin French. A basket of carved blue agate, crisscrossed with platinum pavé-set diamond details that extends to the handle, is filled with an overflowing bouquet of fancy colored diamonds in various cuts and colors.

The Ruban Dentelle necklace was introduced by Van Cleef & Arpels in 2004. Sensual and elegant, it is made with panels of invisibly set Burmese rubies alternating with diamond embroidered flowers from which are suspended pear-shape diamonds.

Right: The petals on this Van Cleef & Arpels brooch, c. 1970, are invisibly set rubies with a cluster of round diamonds in the center. Baguette diamonds form the stem and two marquise-shaped diamonds for leaves. Below: The invisibly set ruby and diamond fuchsia clip brooch and ear clips from 2005 are an adaptation of similarly styled jewels that Van Cleef & Arpels made in the 1960s. Bottom right: The flower head on this rosebud brooch by David Webb is made with cabochon rubies with circular-cut diamonds on the tips of the petals and baguette diamonds encircling the center of the flower. Baguette diamonds form the stem.

The Milly-la-Fôret necklace was designed by Victoire de Castellane for Christian Dior in 2000. It combines leaves of pavé-set emeralds and jade with coral cherries, cabochon ruby raspberries, chalcedony and pearl snow peas, pearl turnips, pavé-set diamond roses, and amethyst flowers.

Jacqueline Karachi-Langane designed this impressive necklace for Cartier, Paris, in 2005. An orchid of pavé-set diamonds and rubies is mounted on three rows of emerald beads and further adorned with cascading emerald leaves decorated with collet-set rubies and accented with ruby drops and diamonds.

In the 1990s Gianmaria Buccellati designed this floral jewelry with the Buccellati characteristic engraving techniques. A pendant brooch with pink gold for the flowers and yellow gold for the leaves and stems is set with diamonds. A large conch pearl hangs from the wreath-like pendant (right). A mountain thistle brooch is set with white and yellow diamonds with a chromo tourmaline at the center of the flower head (below).

Left: This micro-mosaic pendant was created by Laura Hiserote from Vancouver, Washington in 2001. Very fine tesserae depict datura blossom and leaves, a plant that Native Americans use in rite-of-passage ceremonies. Below: These three enameled and diamond-set orchid brooches from 2004 were designed and made by David Freda for Tiffany & Co. They revive the tradition of Paulding Farnham's enameled orchids, dating from 1889.

Notes

Introduction

1   For more information, see Hugh Tait, ed., *Jewelry 7000 Years: An International History and Illustrated Survey from the Collections of the British Museum*, (New York: Harry N. Abrams, Inc., Publishers, 1986), 24.

2   For more information, see Ian Wardropper, et. al., *Renaissance Jewelry in the Alsdorf Collection*, Museum Studies, Vol. 25, no. 2, (Chicago: The Art Institute of Chicago, 2000), 9.

3   For illustration of the Hohenlohe collar, see Ronald W. Lightbown, *Medieval European Jewellery*, (London: Victoria & Albert Museum, 1992), p. 452, pl. 93.

4   For illustrations, see Catherine Cardinal, translated by Jacques Pages, *The Watch from its Origins to the XIXth Century*, (Avon, England: Artline Editons, 1989), p. 133, pl. 98.

5   *Ibid*, p. 124, pl. 87.

6   For illustrations, see Wardropper, *Renaissance Jewelry in the Alsdorf Collection*, 76, 77.

7   This strawberry pendant was presented to Catherine II "The Great" of Russia in 1777 by King Gustav of Sweden when he made a state visit to Russia in that year.

8   For more information, see Clare Phillips, *Jewels and Jewellery*, (London: V&A Publications, 2000), 46.

9   For illustration, see *Ibid.*, 59.

Chapter 1

1   Quoted in Charlotte Gere, *Victorian Jewelry Design*, (Chicago: Henry Regnery Company, 1972), 217–218.

2   As noted in *Ibid.*, 216–227.

3   For more information, see Marguerite Castillon du Perron, translated from the French by Mary McLean, Castillon du Perron, *Princess Mathilde*, Melbourne, (London, Toronto: William Heinemann, Ltd., 1956), 302.

4   For illustration, see Bernard Morel, *The French Crown Jewels: The Objects of the Coronations of the Kings and Queens of France followed by a History of the French Crown Jewels from François I up to the Present Time*, (Bilbao: Fonds Mercator, 1988), 342.

5   Frédéric Boucheron credited Octave Loeulliard for " . . . all my beautiful jewelled flowers. He draws inspiration from nature in the most astonishing way . . . he had made extraordinary accurate leaves and flowers that could not have been more difficult to produce." Quoted in Gilles Néret, *Boucheron: Four Generations of a World-Renowned Jeweler*, (New York: Rizzoli, 1988), 48.

6   Paul Legrand invented the "question mark" closings for these necklaces. *Ibid.*, 47.

7   For illustration, see Susan Weber Soros and Stefanie Walker, eds., *Castellani and Italian Archeological Jewelry*, (New Haven and New York: Bard Graduate Center for Studies in the Decorative Arts, Design, and Culture and Yale University Press, 2004), 228, fig. 9–1.

8   *Ibid.*, Bracelet: 41, fig. 2–13; Brooch: 235, fig. 9–11.

9   *Ibid.*, 242, fig. 9–28.

10   For illustration, see Pier Giovanni Guzzo, *Oreficerie dalla Magna Grecia: ornamenti in oro e argento dall'Italia meridionale tra l'VIII ed il I secolo*, (Taranto: La Colomba, 1993), 99, fig. 52.

11   For illustration, see Hugh Tait, ed., *The Art of the Jeweller: A Catalogue of the Hull Grundy Gift to the British Museum, II: Plates*, (London: British Museum Publications Limited, 1984), Pl. 42, fig. 952.

12   For illustration of a painting by Martin Johnson Heade, *Orchids, Passion Flowers and Hummingbird*, see Jules David Prown, *American Painting: From Its Beginnings to the Armory Show*, (Geneva: Skira, 1969), 72.

13   As cited in Matthew Baigell, *A Concise History of American Painting and Sculpture*, (New York: Harper & Row, Publishers, 1984), 175.

14   *Paris Herald*, September 30, 1889 (clipping from scrapbook IVB, p. 261, Tiffany Archives)

15   Quoted in *Syracuse Herald*, April 7, 1889 (clipping in scrapbook IVA, p. 107, Tiffany Archives).

16   *Ibid.*

17   For illustration, see George Frederick Kunz and Charles Hugh Stevenson, *The Book of the Pearl*, (New York: The Century Co., 1908), facing page 58. Other illustrations in this book included Farnham's pearl jewelry for the 1900 Exposition Universelle in Paris. See facing pages 60, 276.

Chapter 2

1   For more information, see Robert Schmutzler, *Art Nouveau*, (New York: Harry R. Abrams, Inc., Publisher, 1962), 101.

2   Quoted in Vivienne Becker, *Art Nouveau Jewelry*, (New York: E.P. Dutton, 1985), 11.

3   Henri Vever, translated from the French by Katherine Purcell, *French Jewelry of the Nineteenth Century*, (London: Thames & Hudson, 2001), 1151.

4   For illustration of a comb with a leaf partially eaten by insects, see *Ibid.*, 1128, pl. 117.

5   *Ibid*, 1236.

6   Lalique's orchids are so surreal that they almost presage the orchids painted by Georgia O'Keeffe in the 1920s.

7   Vever, *French Jewelry of the Nineteenth Century*, 1246, pl. 126.

8   For illustration, *Ibid.*, 1196, pl. 126. This necklace is in the collection of the Musée des Arts Décoratifs, Paris.

9   For illustration, see Janet Zapata, *The Jewelry and Enamels of Louis Comfort Tiffany*, (New York: Harry N. Abrams, Inc., Publishers, 1993), 79.

10   Quoted from "Tiffany and Company at the Saint Louis Exposition," *The Craftsman*, Vol. VII, no. 2 (November 1904), 182.

11   For illustration, see Zapata, *The Jewelry and Enamels of Louis Comfort Tiffany*, 83.

12   For more information, see Hans Nadelhoffer, *Cartier Jewelers Extraordinary*, (New York: Harry N. Abrams, Inc., Publishers, 1984,) 45–65.

13   For illustration of Fabergé flower brooch with flower jewelry owned by Catherine the Great, see Laura Cerwinske, *Russian Imperial Style*, (New York: Prentice Hall Press, 1990), 93.

Chapter 3

1   Black opals, mined in Australia, were not customarily a gemstone used by fine jewelers. It was a stone most often associated with artistically

inspired designers such as Louis Comfort Tiffany. Marcus & Co. was also noted for creating imaginative jewelry with black opals.

2   For illustration of door a from Willow Tea-Room, see Robert Schmutzler, *Art Nouveau*, (New York: Harry N. Abrams, Inc., Publishers: 1962), 243.

3   Quoted in Judy Rudoe, *Cartier 1900–1939*, (New York: Harry N. Abrams, Inc., Publishers, 1997), 210, no. 2.

4   For more information, see François Chaille, based on notes and writings by Éric Nussbaum, *The Cartier Collection, Jewelry*, (Paris, Flammarion, 2004), 188.

5   For illustration of brooches and bracelets, see Henri Clouzot, "La Parure à l'Exposition des Arts Décoratifs," *La Renaissance de L'Art Français et des Industries de Luxe*, (January 1926, Vol. 9, no. 1), 41.

6   For illustration of bracelet and brooch as well as a another bracelet with a garland of flowers, see Geo. Bloch, Ivanhoé Rambosson, Isy de Botton, P. Contreau, and G. Fouquet, *Le Grand Négoce: Expostion des Arts Décoratifs 1925*, (Paris: L'Imprimerie de Vaugirard, March 15, 1926), 40. I would like to thank Ulysses G. Dietz for showing me this catalogue.

Chapter 4

1   Cited in Paul E. Flato, Inc., advertisement, *Harper's Bazaar*, May 1934, 112.

2   According to Thomas Heyman at Oscar Heyman & Brothers, the first two gardenias were finished on March 17, 1936 and were sold for $1,394.44 each.

3   According to T. Heyman, the first pansy was finished on August 31, 1936 and was sold to Udall & Ballou for $750.

4   Quoted in Caroline Childers, *Rainbow of Jewelry*, (New York: BW Publishing Associates, Inc. and Rizzoli International Publications, Inc., 2000), 223

5   For illustration of Norman Shearer wearing the ivy necklace, see Annette Tapert, *The Power of Glamour*, (London: Aurum Press, Ltd., 1999), 81.

6   For illustration, see John Loring, *Tiffany's 20th Century: A Portrait of American Style*, (New York:

Harry N. Abrams, Inc., Publishers, 1997), 113.

7   For illustration of Daisy Fellowes wearing the Boivin orchid, see "Baubles," *Vogue*, (January 15, 1936), 71.

8   As noted in Françoise Cailles, translated by Tanya Leslie, *René Boivin: Jeweller*, (London: Quartet Books, 1994), 224, 229.

9   I would like to thank Nico Landrigan for pointing this out to me.

Chapter 5

1   Éric Nussbaum, the former curator of the Cartier Collection, noted that this palm tree " . . . was one of the most important items in the Cartier Collection, given the extraordinary quality of the rubies (supplied by the client), its baguette-cut diamonds set in platinum, and its elegant execution." As quoted in François Chaille, based on notes and writings of Éric Nussbaum, *The Cartier Collection; Jewelry*, (Paris: Flammarion, 2004), 313.

2   For more information, see Daniela Mascetti and Amanda Triossi, *Bulgari*, (Milan: Leonardo, 1996), 80–81.

3   For preliminary drawings of dahlia brooch, see Viviane Jutheau, *Sterlé: Joaillier Paris*, (Paris: Éditions Vecteurs, 1990), pages not numbered.

4   Quoted in A. Kenneth Snowman, ed., "Tiffany," *The Master Jewelers*, (London: Thames and Hudson, Ltd., 188.

5   The flowers on the "Hedges and Rows" necklace could also be some undefined underwater sea creature, according to Pierce Maguire, director of Schlumberger at Tiffany & Co. I would like to thank him for identifying the Schlumberger jewelry.

6   Christmas-tree jewelry first appeared in costume jewelry at the end of the Second World War. They were referred to as "fur pins" since they were often attached to fur collars, mink hats, or stoles. For examples of Christmas-tree jewelry, see Gabriella Mariotti, *All My Baskets: American Costume Jewelry 1930—1960*, (Milan: Franco Maria Ricci, 1996), 64–70.

Chapter 6

1   See Christie's sale, *The Contemporary Jeweler*, October 26, 2000, which featured jewelry by Cecilia Rodrigues, Gioia, Martin Katz, Aletto Brothers, William Goldberg, Fred Leighton, James de Givenchy, De Grisogono, Michelle Ong, Lynn Nakamura, Bhagat, and Ralph Esmerian.

2   As quoted in *Tiffany & Co. 1979–1980*, (New York: Tiffany & Co., 1979), 33.

3   As quoted in Penny Proddow and Marion Fasel, *Bejeweled: Great Designers, Celebrity Style*, (New York: Harry N. Abrams, Inc., Publishers, 2001, 132.

4   Quoted in Vivienne Becker, "House of the Rising Scion," *Harpers & Queen*, October 2003. (from Taffin publicity files)

5   Quoted in Johanna Dormer, *Stefan Hemmerle: Art of Nature*, (New York: Stefan Hemmerle, nd), 7.

6   Cacholong is a cream-colored opal lacking fire. Some sources claim it is an opaque chalcedony.

7   For illustration of necklace, see *Harpers Bazaar*, March 15, 1938, 59.

8   Quoted in Website, fashionwindows.com/fashion_designers/dior/victoire de castellane, 1.

9   The datura is a plant used in rite of passage ceremonies by Native Americans.

Selected Bibliography

Aldred, Cyril, *Jewels of the Pharaohs*, New York, Washington: Praeger Publishers, Inc., 1991.

Andrews, Carol, *Ancient Egyptian Jewelry*, New York: Harry N. Abrams, Inc., Publishers, 1991.

Arpels, Jacques, Catherine Join-Dieterle, Fabienne Falluel, Liesel Couvreue-Schiffer, and Marie-France Lary, *Van Cleef & Arpels*, Paris: Diffusion Paris-Musées, 1992.

Becker, Vivienne, *Art Nouveau Jewelry*, New York: E. P. Dutton, 1985.

——, *Antique and Twentieth Century Jewellery: A Guide for Collectors*, 2nd ed., Colchester, Essex: N.A.G. Press, Ltd., 1987.

Bennett, David and Daniela Mascetti, *Understanding Jewellery*, Woodbridge, Suffolk: Antique Collectors' Club, 1994.

Brunhammer, Yvonne, ed., *The Jewels of Lalique*, Paris, New York: Flammarion, 1988.

Buccellati, Maria Cristina Buccellati, ed., *Buccellati: Art in Gold, Silver and Gems*, Milan: Skira Editore S.p.A., 2000.

Bury, Shirley, *Jewellery 1789–1910: The International Era*, 2 vols., Woodbridge, Suffolk: Antique Collectors' Club, 1991.

Cailles, François, translated by Tanya Leslie, *René Boivin, Jeweller*, London: Quartet Books Limited, 1994.

Chaille, François, based on notes and writings by Éric Nussbaum, *The Cartier Collection: Jewelry*, Paris: Flammarion, 2004.

Childers, Caroline, *Rainbow of Jewelry*, New York: BW Publishing Associates, Inc. and Rizzoli International Publications, Inc., 2000.

Cologni, Franco and Eric Nussbaum, *Platinum by Cartier: Triumphs of the Jewelers' Art*, New York: Harry N. Abrams, Inc., Publishers, 1996.

Corbett, Patricia, *Verdura: The Life and Work of a Master Jeweler*, New York: Harry N. Abrams, Inc., Publishers, 2002.

Corgnati, Martina, *Mario Buccellati: Prince of Goldsmiths*, New York: Rizzoli International Publications, Inc., 1998.

De Cerval, Marguerite, *Mauboussin*, Paris: Éditions du Regard, 1992.

Despini, Aikaterini, *Greek Art: Ancient Gold Jewellery*, Athens: Ekdotike Athenon S.A., 1996.

Dietz, Ulysses Grant, Jenna Weissman Joselit, Kevin J. Smead, and Janet Zapata, *The Glitter and the Gold: Fashioning America's Jewelry*, Newark: The Newark Museum, 1997.

Everitt, Sally and David Lancaster, *Christie's Twentieth-Century Jewelry*, New York: Watson-Guptill Publications, 2002.

Fales, Martha Gandy, *Jewelry in America 1600–1900*, Woodbridge, Suffolk: Antique Collectors' Club, 1995.

Gabardi, Melissa, *Art Deco Jewellery 1920–1949*, Woodbridge, Suffolk: Antique Collectors' Club, 1989.

——, translated by Solange Schnall, *Les Bijoux des Années 50*, Milan: Éditions de L'Amateur, 1987.

——, translated by Diana Scarisbrick, *Gioielli Anni '40: The Jewels of the 1940s in Europe*, Milan: Gruppo Giorgio Mondadori, 1982.

Garside, Anne, ed., *Jewelry, Ancient to Modern*, New York, Baltimore: The Viking Press in cooperation with the Walters Art Gallery, 1980.

Gary, Marie-Noël de, Evelyne Possémé, Marc Bascou, Yvonne Brunhammer, Yvonne Deslandres, Charlotte Gere, and François Mathey, *Les Fouquets: Bijoutiers et Joailliers à Paris 1860–1960*, Paris: Musée des Arts Décoratifs and Flammarion, 1983.

Gere, Charlotte, *Victorian Jewelry Design*, Chicago: Henry Regnery Company, 1973.

—— and Geoffrey C. Munn, *Artists' Jewellery: Pre-Raphaelite to Arts and Crafts*, Woodbridge, Suffolk: Antique Collectors' Club, 1989.

Hackenbroch, Yvonne, *Renaissance Jewellery*, London: Sotheby Parke Bernet Publications by Philip Wilson Publishers, Ltd., 1979.

Hapsburg, Géza von, *Fabergé in America*, London and San Francisco: Thames & Hudson, Ltd. and Fine Arts Museums of San Francisco, 1996.

Jutheau, Viviane, *Sterlé: Joaillier Paris*, Paris, Éditions Vecteurs, 1990.

Koch, Michael, Evelyne Possémé, Judy Rudoe, Geoffrey Munn, Marie-Noël de Gary, Barbara Furrer, Cathérine Arminjon, and Alexander Herzog von Württemberg, *The Belle Epoque of French Jewellery: Jewellery Making in Paris 1850–1910*, London: Thomas Heneage & Co., Ltd, 1990.

Krashes, Lawrence and Ronald Winston, ed., *Harry Winston: The Ultimate Jeweler*, New York and Santa Monica: Harry Winston, Inc. and the Gemological Institute of America, 1984.

Loring, John, *Louis Comfort Tiffany at Tiffany & Co.*, New York: Harry N. Abrams, Inc., Publishers, 2002.

——, *Paulding Farnham: Tiffany's Lost Genius*, New York: Harry N. Abrams, Inc., Publishers, 2000.

——, *Tiffany Flora/Tiffany Fauna*, New York: Harry N. Abrams, Inc., Publishers, 2003.

——, *Tiffany Jewels*, New York: Harry N. Abrams, Inc., Publishers, 1999.

Mascetti, Daniela and Amanda Triossi, *Bulgari*, Milan: Leonardo, 1996.

——, *Earrings: From Antiquity to the Present*, New York: Rizzoli International Publications, Inc., 1990.

——, *The Necklace: From Antiquity to the Present*, New York: Harry N. Abrams, Inc., Publishers, 1997.

McConnell, Sophie, *Metropolitan Jewelry*, New York, Boston, Toronto, London: The Metropolitan Museum of Art and A Bulfinch Press Book/Little, Brown and Company, 1991.

Munn, Geoffrey C., *Castellani and Giuliano: Revivalist Jewellers of the 19th Century*, New York:

Rizzoli International Publications, Inc., 1984.

———, *The Triumph of Love: Jewelry 1530–1930*, London: Thames & Hudson, 1993.

———, *Tiaras: A History of Splendour*, Woodbridge, Suffolk: Antique Collectors' Club, 2001.

Nadelhoffer, Hans, *Cartier: Jewelers Extraordinary*, New York: Harry N. Abrams, Inc., Publishers, 1984.

Néret, Gilles, *Boucheron: Four Generations of a World-Renowned Jeweler*, New York: Rizzoli International Publications, Inc., 1988.

Phillips, Clare, *Jewels and Jewellery*, London: V&A Publications, 2000.

Proddow, Penny and Debra Healy, *American Jewelry: Glamour and Tradition*, New York: Rizzoli International Publications, Inc., 1987.

—— and Marion Fasel, *Bejeweled: Great Designers, Celebrity Style*, New York: Harry N. Abrams, Inc., Publishers, 2001.

———, *Diamonds: A Century of Spectacular Jewels*, New York: Harry N. Abrams, Inc., Publishers, 1996.

Purcell, Katherine, *Falize: A Dynasty of Jewelers*, London: Thames and Hudson, 1999.

Raulet, Sylvie, translated by Lucinda Gane, *Art Deco Jewelry*, New York: Rizzoli International Publications, Inc., 1985.

———, translated by Steward Spencer, *Jewelry of the 1940s and 1950s*, New York: Rizzoli International Publications, Inc., 1988.

———, *Van Cleef & Arpels*, New York: Rizzoli International Publications, Inc., 1987.

Rosenthal, Joel, *JAR Paris*, London: Art Books International, 2002.

Rudoe, Judy, *Cartier 1900–1939*, New York: Harry N. Abrams, Inc., Publishers and The Metropolitan Museum of Art, 1997.

Scarisbrick, Diana, *Ancestral Jewels*, London: André Deutsch Limited, 1989.

———, *Tiara*, San Francisco and Boston: Chronicle Books in association with the Museum of Fine Arts, Boston, 2000.

Schadt, Hermann, *Goldsmiths' Art: 5000 Years of Jewelry and Hollowware*, Stuttgart: Arnoldsche, 1996.

Snowman, Kenneth, A., ed., *The Master Jewelers*, London: Thames and Hudson, 1990.

Soros, Susan Weber and Stefanie Walker, eds., *Castellani and Italian Archeological Jewelry*, New Haven and New York: The Bard Graduate Center for Studies in the Decorative Arts, Design, and Culture and Yale University Press, 2004.

Tait, Hugh, ed. *The Art of the Jeweller: A Catalogue of the Hull Grundy Gift to the British Museum, I: Text II: Plates*, London: British Museum Publications Limited, 1984.

Traina, John with foreword by Danielle Steele, *Extraordinary Jewels*, New York: Doubleday, 1994.

Vaill, Amanda and Janet Zapata, *Seaman Schepps: A Century of New York Jewelry Design*, New York: The Vendome Press, 2004.

Vever, Henri, translated from the French by Katherine Purcell, *French Jewelry of the Nineteenth Century*, London: Thames and Hudson, 2001.

Zapata, Janet, *The Art of Zadora: America's Fabergé*, New York: The Vendome Press, 1999.

———, *The Jewelry and Enamels of Louis Comfort Tiffany*, New York: Harry N. Abrams, Inc., Publishers, 1993.

———, with Anna Tobin D'Ambrosio and contributions by Jonathan Snellenberg and Ricardo Zapata, *Jewels of Time: Watches from the Munson-Williams-Proctor Arts Institute*, Utica: Munson-Williams-Proctor Arts Institute, 2001.

Credits

Listed by page number

1: Private collection, photo © GIA and Tino Hammid

4–5: Neil Lane, Los Angeles

6: The Metropolitan Museum of Art, Dodge Fund, 1933; Photo © 1983 The Metropolitan Museum of Art

8 all: The Walters Art Museum, Baltimore

9: Toledo Museum of Art, Greek, gift of the Apollo Society, Oak Leaf Wreath (1987.3 a-f); Photo by Tim Thayer, 1996

10 all: Diamond Fund, Kremlin, Moscow

11 right: Diamond Fund, Kremlin, Moscow. Left: Sandra Cronan, Ltd., London

12: Munson-Williams-Proctor Arts Institute, Museum of Art, Utica, New York, photo by John Bigelow Taylor

13 right: Wartski, London. Left all: The Walters Art Museum, Baltimore, collection of Henry Walters, gift of Laura F. Delano, 1946-47

14: Toledo Museum of Art, purchased with funds given by Rita Barbour Kern, 1996.27.

16 all: Wartski, London

17 all: James Robinson, New York

18: Private collection, photo © 2006 David Behl

19: Metropolitan Opera Guild, photo © 1996 David Behl

20: Fred Leighton, New York

21: Boucheron archives, Paris

23 top: Fred Leighton, New York. Middle: Nan Summerfield, Beverly Hills. Bottom: Sotheby's

24: Boucheron archives, Paris

25: Thomas Faerber S.A., Geneva, photo © Katharina Faerber

26: James Robinson, New York

27 top left: Neil Lane, Los Angeles, photo by Richard Rubins. Right: Veronique Bamps, Brussels. Lower left: James Robinson, New York. Drawings: Mauboussin archives, Paris

28: Wartski, London

29 top: © 2003 Doris Duke Charitable Foundation, photo by Richard Walker. Right: James Robinson, New York

30–31: Sotheby's

32 left: Sotheby's. Upper right: James Robinson, New York

33 all: Sotheby's

34 all: Wartski, London

35 all: James Robinson, New York

36: Neil Lane, Los Angeles, photo by Richard Rubins

37 all: James Robinson, New York

38 all: Private collection

39 upper right: Wartski, London. Lower right: Private collection. Lower left: Courtesy Tiffany & Co. archives, photo © David Lawrence

40 upper left: Sotheby's. Lower right: Vartanian & Sons, Inc., New York, photo © 2006 David Behl

41 upper left: Courtesy Tiffany & Co. archives, photo © Carlton Davis. Lower right: S. J. Phillips, London

42: G. Torroni, S.A., Geneva

43 left: Primavera Gallery, New York. Right: The Walters Art Museum, Baltimore

44: Collection of The Newark Museum, gift of Herman A. E. and Paul C. Jaehne, 1941 41.725

47 top: Sotheby's. Bottom: Ulf Breede, Berlin

48: Neil Lane, Los Angeles

51: Private collection, photo © 1998 David Behl

52: Macklowe Gallery, New York

53: Private collection, photo © 1998 David Behl

54 top: © 2006 Christie's Images LTD. Bottom: Vartanian & Sons, Inc., New York, photo © 2006 David Behl

55: Private collection, photo © 1998 David Behl

56 left: Ernst Färber, Munich. Right: Toledo Museum of Art, Mr. and Mrs. George M. Jones, Jr. Fund, 1995.13, photo © 1999 Tim Thayer

57: Private collection

58: © 2006 Christie's Images LTD

59 top: Pierre Bergé & Associates, Paris. Bottom: © 2006 Christie's Images LTD

60 top left: Janet Mavec, New York. Bottom: The Metropolitan Museum of Art, gift of Mrs. J.G. Phelps Stokes [née Lettic L. Sands], 1965 (6515ab); Photo by Bobby Hansson, © 1988 The Metropolitan Museum of Art

61 top: Ira Simon collection, photo by Michael Tropea. Left: © Louis C. Tiffany Garden Museum, Japan. Right: Macklowe Gallery, New York

62: Toledo Museum of Art, purchased with funds given by Rita Barbour Kern, 1996.1, photo by Tim Thayer 1996

63 top: Toledo Museum of Art, Mr. and Mrs. George M. Jones, Jr. Fund, 2003.19. Right: Van Cleef & Arpels collection, Paris. Left bottom: Nan Summerfield and Anne Marie Stanton, Beverly Hills

64–65: The Cartier Collection, © Cartier

66 top left: A La Vieille Russie, New York. Top right: Ernst Färber, Munich. Bottom: Private collection

67 top: Boucheron archives, Paris. Bottom: Fred Leighton, New York

68: Private collection, photo © 2006 David Behl

69 top and bottom left: The Cartier Collection, photo © 1987 David Behl. Right: Cartier archives, © Cartier

70: Private collection, photo © GIA and Tino Hammid

72 top: Neil Lane, Los Angeles. Left: Vartanian & Sons, Inc., New York, photo © 2006 David Behl. Bottom: Primavera Gallery, New York

73: © 2006 Christie's Images LTD

74 top and lower right: The Cartier Collection, © Cartier. Left: Pierre Bergé & Associates, Paris

75 top left: The Cartier Collection, © Cartier. All others: The Mauboussin archives, Paris

76 top: Courtesy of Historical Design, Inc., New York, from the Richard H. Driehaus Collection, photo by Michael Tropea. Left both: Stephen-Russell, New York

77: Private collection, photo © GIA and Tino Hammid

78: Private collection, photo © 1987 David Behl

79 top all: © 2006 Christie's Images LTD. Bottom: Sotheby's

80: Sotheby's

81 top: Stephen-Russell, New York. Middle: Sotheby's. Bottom: Van Cleef & Arpels, Paris

82 left: Private collection, photo © GIA and Tino Hammid. Right: Sotheby's

83 top: Sotheby's. Middle: Janet Mavec, New York. Bottom: © 2006 Christie's Images LTD

84 top: The Cartier Collection, © Cartier. Middle and bottom: © 2006 Christie's Images LTD.

85: The Cartier Collection, © Cartier, photo by N. Welsh

86 left: Van Cleef & Arpels archives. Right: Van Cleef & Arpels, Paris

87 left: Firestone & Parson Jewelers, Boston. Right: Van Cleef & Arpels archives

88: © 2006 Christie's Images LTD

90: Nelson Rarities, Portland, Maine, photo © Stretch Studios. All rights reserved.

91: Sotheby's

92: © 2006 Christie's Images LTD

93: The Cartier Collection, © Cartier

94: © 2006 Christie's Images LTD

95 left: Cartier archives, © Cartier. Right: The Cartier Collection, © Cartier

96: The Cartier Collection, © Cartier

97: Private collection, photo © GIA and Tino Hammid

98 top: Boucheron archives, Paris. Bottom: Private collection, photo © GIA and Tino Hammid

99: Sotheby's

100 right: Van Cleef & Arpels archives, Paris. Left: Boucheron archives. Bottom: Private collection, photo © GIA and Tino Hammid

101 left and top: Van Cleef & Arpels, Paris. Bottom right: Van Cleef & Arpels archives, Paris

102 top: Oscar Heyman & Brothers, New York. Left: Private collection, photo © GIA and Tino Hammid. Bottom: Van Cleef & Arpels, Paris

103 left top: Vartanian & Sons., Inc., New York, photo © 2006 David Behl. Bottom left: Veronique Bamps, Brussels. Right: Sotheby's

104: Mauboussin archives, Paris

105 left: Oscar Heyman & Brothers, New York. Right: Private collection. Bottom: Vartanian & Sons, Inc., New York, photo © Zane White

106: Private collection

107 left: Van Cleef & Arpels archives, Paris. Right: Van Cleef & Arpels collection, Paris

108 left: Private collection, photo © 2006 David Behl. Right: Private collection

109 top: Oscar Heyman & Brothers, New York. Left: Van Cleef & Arpels collection, Paris. Right: Private collection, photo © 2006 David Behl

110 top left: Private collection, photo © 2006 David Behl. Top right: Boucheron archives, Paris. Bottom: Neil Lane, Los Angeles

111 top: Tiffany & Co., photo © Kenro Izu. Left: Camilla Dietz Bergeron, Ltd., New York. Right: Private collection, photo © Steven Rothfeld

112 left: Boucheron archives, Paris. Right: James Robinson, New York. Bottom: Toledo Museum of Art, gift of Rhoda L. and Roger M. Berkowitz, 2004.14

113: Boucheron archives, Paris

114: © 2006 Christie's Images LTD

115 left: The Cartier Collection © Cartier. Right: Richters of Palm Beach

116 top: Private collection, photo © GIA and Tino Hammid. Left bottom: Verdura, New York. Right bottom: Primavera Gallery, New York

117 upper right: © 2006 Christie's Images LTD. All others: Sotheby's

118: Photo courtesy of Martin du Daffoy, Paris

119 left: The Cartier Collection © Cartier, photo by N. Welsh. Middle and right: The Cartier Collection © Cartier

120: Van Cleef & Arpels archives, Paris

121: Private collection, photo © GIA and Tino Hammid

122 top: The Cartier Collection © Cartier. Left: Hancocks, London. Right: Camilla Dietz Bergeron, Ltd., New York

123 top: Sotheby's. Left: Primavera Gallery, New York. Right: Pierre Bergé & Associates, Paris. Bottom: Veronique Bamps, Brussels

124 top: Private collection, photo © 2006 David Behl. Middle and bottom: Seaman Schepps, New York

125 top: Courtesy Tiffany & Co. archives. Bottom: Seaman Schepps, New York

126 left: Private collection, photo © 2006 David Behl. Right: The Cartier Collection © Cartier, photo by N. Welsh

127: © 2006 Christie's Images LTD

128: Courtesy Tiffany & Co. archives

130–131 all: Private collection, photo © GIA and Tino Hammid

132. Mauboussin archives, Paris

133. Private collection, photo by Steven Rothfeld

134 left: Millon & Associés, Paris. Right: Private collection

135 top: © 2006 Christie's Images LTD. Right: Villa Gioielliere, Milan. Left: Vartanian & Sons, Inc., New York, photo © 2006 David Behl

136: Mauboussin archives, Paris

137: Private collection, photo © GIA and Tino Hammid

138 all: Private collection, photo © GIA and Tino Hammid

139: Vartanian & Sons, Inc., New York, photo © 2006 David Behl

140–141: Private collection, photo © GIA and Tino Hammid

142: Firestone & Parsons Jewelers, Boston

143: Van Cleef & Arpels collection, Paris

144: Private collection, photo © GIA and Tino Hammid

145 left: Van Cleef & Arpels archives, Paris. Center: Van Cleef & Arpels, Paris. Right: Private collection, photo © GIA and Tino Hammid

146 all: Cartier archives, © Cartier

147: Richters of Palm Beach

148 top: © 2006 Christie's Images LTD. Left: Gary Hansen, St. Louis. Right: © 2006 Christie's Images LTD

149 left: The Cartier Collection, © Cartier. Right: © 2006 Christie's Images LTD

150: Maison Duhem, Paris

151 top and right: Photo courtesy of Bvlgari Historical Archive, Rome. Left: Richters of Palm Beach.

152: Primavera Gallery, New York

153 top: Courtesy Tiffany & Co. archives. Left: © 2006 Christie's Images LTD. Right: Verdura, New York

154–155: Private collection, photo © GIA and Tino Hammid

156 left: Primavera Gallery, New York. Center: Private collection, photo © GIA and Tino Hammid. Right: Tiffany & Co., photo © Carlton David

157 top and left: Private collection, photo © GIA and Tino Hammid. Right: © 2006 Christie's Images LTD

158 left: Verdura, New York. Right: Primavera Gallery, New York

159 left: Courtesy Tiffany & Co. Right: Primavera Gallery, New York

160: Van Cleef & Arpels, Paris

161 left: Verdura, New York. Right: Sotheby's

162 top: Gary Hansen, St. Louis. Left: Sotheby's. Right: Camilla Dietz Bergeron, Ltd., New York

163: Toledo Museum of Art, purchased with funds provided by Rita Barbour Kern and funds given by the family and friends of Phyllis Fox Driggs, 1999.3, photo by Tim Thayer 1999

164 all: Verdura, Inc., photo © 1993 David Behl

165 left: Maison Duhem, Paris. Right: Verdura, New York. Bottom: Oscar Heyman & Brothers, New York

166: © 2006 Christie's Images LTD

168 left: Richters of Palm Beach. Bottom: Sotheby's

169 top: The Cartier Collection, © Cartier. Bottom: Sotheby's

170: Sotheby's

171: Patrizia Ferenczi, New York

172: © 2006 Christie's Images LTD

173: Boucheron archives, Paris

174 all: Maison Duhem, Paris

175: Bvlgari, Rome

176 left: Chanel, Paris. Right: Ellagem, New York

177 left and middle: Oscar Heyman & Brothers, New York. Right: Fred Leighton, New York

178 all: Hemmerle, Munich

179: © 2006 Christie's Images LTD

180 top: © 2006 Christie's Images LTD. Left: Sotheby's. Bottom: Marilyn Cooperman, New York

181: Marilyn Cooperman, New York

182: Oscar Heyman & Brothers, New York, photo © 2006 David Behl

183: Sotheby's

184 top: Neil Lane, Los Angeles. Bottom: Harry Winston, New York

185 left: Kazanjian Brothers, Beverly Hills. Right: Asprey London

186 left: Martin Katz, Beverly Hills. Middle: Van Cleef & Arpels, Paris. Right: Private collection

187: Sotheby's

188: © 2006 Christie's Images LTD

189: Private collection, photo © Katharina Faerber

190 top: Sorab & Roshi, Cross River, New York. Bottom and right: Christopher Walling, New York. Left: James de Givenchy for Taffin, New York

191 right: Verdura, New York. Left: Private collection, photo © 2006 David Behl.

192: Linda Goldstein for Henry Dunay, New York

193 all: James de Givenchy for Taffin, New York

194 left: Christopher Walling, New York. Right: Martin Katz, Beverly Hills

195–197 all: Hemmerle, Munich

198 all: Oscar Heyman & Brothers, New York

199 left: Villa Gioielliere, Milan. Right: Oscar Heyman & Brothers, New York

200: Andreas von Zadora-Gerlof, photo © 1999 David Behl

201: Sotheby's

202: Harry Winston, New York

203: © 2006 Christie's Images LTD

204: Van Cleef & Arpels, Paris

205 left: Van Cleef & Arpels, Paris. Right: © 2006 Christie's Images LTD. Top: Sotheby's

206: Christian Dior, Paris

207: Cartier, Paris

208 all: Buccellati Milan Historical Archive

209 left: © Hiserote Micromosaic, 2001, photo by Erica and Harold Van Pelt. Right: Tiffany & Co., photo © David Lawrence

Endpapers: Verdura, New York

Acknowledgments

A book is always the sum of all those who made it possible. We want to thank our friends and associates who provided photography or helped answer our myriad of questions. We are especially indebted to our husbands who, quite frankly, put up with us as we worked through the intricacies of the book. They each deserve two flowers; a red rose, which signifies our love for them and a bluebell for their constancy.

Special people along the way made our journey a bit easier. Jennifer Guadagno helped with transcribing notes. The photographers David Behl and Tino Hammid turned precious metal and gemstones into flowers, fruits, vegetables, trees, or leaves that seem almost as if they were alive. The staff at The Vendome Press were patient and helpful: we would like to thank Sarah Davis, who seemed to do everything; Mark Magowan, whose calm demeanor helped smooth ruffled feathers; and Alexis Gregory, who kept the tenor of the book on a high pitch. Special thanks also to our graphic designer, Judy Hudson, at Biproduct.

Many jewelry concerns were helpful with images of their most important pieces. We would like to thank the following: Howard M. Hyde, Asprey-Garrard, New York; Michel Tonnelot, Boucheron, Paris; Silvia McGinley, Buccellati, New York; Krista Florin, Bulgari, New York and Amanda Triossi, Bulgari, Rome; Michel Aliaga and Pierre Raniero, Cartier International, Paris; Vanessa Bongrand, Chanel, Paris; Anne Charrier, Christian Dior, Paris; Tom Heyman, Rhonda Castellani, and the artisans at Oscar Heyman & Brothers, New York; Marguerite De Cerval and Béatrice Rosenthal, Mauboussin, Paris; Anthony Hopenhajm, Seaman Schepps, New York; Annamarie Sandecki, Louisa Bann, Linda Buckley, and Pierce B. MacGuire, Tiffany & Co., Parsippany, New Jersey and New York; Ward Landrigan and Nico Landrigan, Verdura, Inc., New York; Catherine Cariou, Van Cleef & Arpels, Paris; Stanley Silberstein, David Webb, New York; and Tracy Bliven, Harry Winston, New York.

Gallery owners from around the world were helpful in finding great jewelry to illustrate in our book. The following provided us with illustrative material: Veronique Bamps, Brussels; Camilla Dietz Bergeron and Gus Davis, Camilla Dietz Bergeron, Ltd., New York; Ulf Breede, Berlin; Sandra Cronan and Catherine Taylor, Sandra Cronan, Ltd., London; Jean-Luc and Bénédicte de Foucaud, Martin du Daffoy, Paris; Ernst Färber, Munich; Lydia Stonborough and Thomas Faerber, Thomas Faerber S.A., Geneva; Patrizia Ferenczi, New York; David Firestone, Firestone and Parson, Boston; Stephen Burton, Hancocks & Co., Ltd., London; Gary Hansen, Hansen Minerals, St. Louis; Denis Gallion and Daniel Morris, Historical Design, Inc., New York; Michael Kazanjian, Kazanjian Bros., Beverly Hills; Neil Lane, Neil Lane Jewelry, Los Angeles; Fred Leighton, Fred Leighton Rare Collectible Jewels, New York; Barbara Macklowe and Benjamin Macklowe, Macklowe Gallery and Modernism, New York; Janet Mavec, New York; Andrew Nelson, Malcolm Logan, and David Johanson, Nelson Rarities, Inc., Portland, Maine; Jonathan Norton, S.J. Phillips, London; Audrey Friedman, Primavera Gallery, New York; Stefan Richter, Richter's, Palm Beach; Frederick L. Gray and Mark Collins, Richter's, Atlanta; Joan Munves-Boeing and Helene Kreniske, James Robinson, Inc., New York; Lee Siegelson, Susan Abeles, and Jeanette Quindoy, Siegelson, Inc., New York; Stephen Feuerman and Russell Zelenetz, Stephen-Russell, New York; Anne-Marie Stanton, Beverly Hills; Nan Summerfield, Beverly Hills; Virginie Torroni and Guiseppe Torroni, G. Torroni, S.A., Geneva; Paul Vartanian and Nishan Vartanian, Vartanian & Sons, Inc., New York; Peter Schaffer, À La Vieille Russie, New York; and Geoffrey C. Munn, Katherine Purcell, and Sophia Dicks, Wartski, London.

The book was aided by contemporary jewelers who contributed images of their wonderful creations, destined to be tomorrow's treasures. These include Sorab and Roshi Bouzarjomehri, Cross River, New York; Marilyn Cooperman, New York; Henry Dunay, Henry Designs, Inc., New York; Ella and Talila Gafter, Ellagem, New York; David Freda, San Clemente; James de Givenchy, Taffin, New York; Stefan Hemmerle, Hemmerle, Munich; Laura Hiserote, Vancouver, Washington; Jay Carlile and Martin Katz, Martin Katz, Ltd., Los Angeles; Filippo Villa, Villa Gioielliere, Milan; Christopher Walling, Christopher Walling, Inc., New York; and Andrea von Zadora-Gerlof, Zadora, New York and London.

Museums have collected important botanical jewelry and we would like to thank the following for supplying us with images: Elizabeth E. Steinberg, Doris Duke Charitable Foundation, Somerville, New Jersey; Robert Tuggle, Metropolitan Opera Guild, New York; Julie Zeftel, Metropolitan Museum of Art, New York; Anna D'Ambrosio, Munson-Williams-Proctor Arts Institute, Utica; Ulysses G. Dietz and William Peniston, The Newark Museum; Takeo Horiuchi and Takashi Horiuchi, Louis C. Tiffany Garden Museum, Matsue, Japan; Jutta Page, Patricia Whitesides and Nicole Rivette, Toledo Museum of Art; and Michael Gunn, Walters Art Museum, Baltimore.

We are indebted to the auction houses for supplying numerous images of some of the most important pieces in the book. We thank Debbie Bloom, Christie's; Valérie Sammut, Millon & Associates, Paris; Lisa Hubbard, Yvonne Teng, Carol Elkins, and Alexandra Rhodes, Sotheby's; and Frédéric Chambre and Eric Buffetaud, Pierre Bergé & Associates, Paris.

We would also like to thank the following who either provided us with images, answered questions, or were supportive in some way: Alain Cartier, London and Paris; Richard H. Driehaus and Maureen Devine, Driehaus Enterprise Management, Chicago; Jean-Claude Duhem and Pierre-Édouard Duhem, Paris; Linda Goldstein of Linda Goldstein Public Relations, New York; Elise B. Misiorowski, Gemological Institute of America, Carlsbad, California; Dr. Joseph and Ruth Sataloff, and Ira Simon.

Suzanne Tennenbaum
Janet Zapata

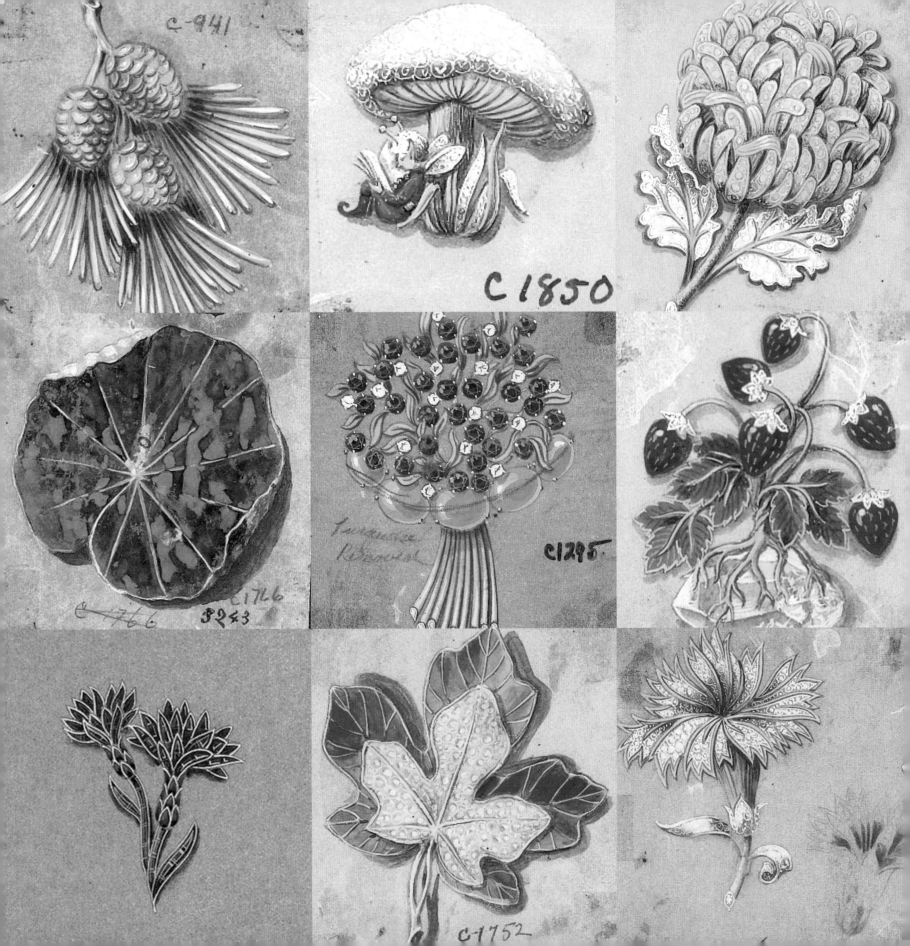